Could It Be True?

What The Evidence Says About God and What It Means For Us

Jack Duga

Could It Be True?

Praise for "Could It Be True?"

"In *Could It Be True?*, Jack Duga opens his heart and shares the deeply personal journey that led him into a life-changing relationship with Jesus Christ. Jack is a kind and caring man whose genuine love for others is evident on every page, as he thoughtfully answers common objections to the Christian faith while pointing readers to the solid foundation for belief he discovered. More than just a defense of faith, this book is his invitation for others to experience the same hope, forgiveness, and transformation that God has graciously brought into his own life."

- Robby Bolden, Director of Pastoral Care, Care for Pastors.

"Jack first came on my radar at our church because he was consistently sharing his faith with people who don't know Christ–I kept hearing about it from others. That's what led me to bring him onto our staff, and it's the same evangelistic drive that now shows up in this book. What he's been faithfully doing out loud, he's now put into writing, and I'm glad to recommend both him and this work."

- Michael Sorcinelli, Founding and Lead Pastor, New Day Church

Could It Be True?

Published by Methuselah Publishing.

Cover design by Jacob Duga

To Dad

CONTENTS

Introduction

My Story

My faith story began in 2017. I was 18 years old and worked at the town movie theater. I loved working at the theater, because there was this really cute girl who worked with me. Her name was Lizzy. (And, as a matter of fact, it still is!) I would normally try to pick up a few extra shifts at work each week, not for the money, but because I wanted to work while Lizzy was working.

As you can imagine, slow days at work were the best, because I could largely just stand around and talk to Lizzy for most of my shift. And, luckily for me, our movie theater was the slowest in the area. So slow, in fact, that it ended up closing down just five years after I left my job there. It's not that I didn't like work, I did work hard while I was there, and I enjoyed it. But one would be a fool to think that I wouldn't take advantage of the slow days.

Well, on one of these slow days, Lizzy's dad, Barry, decided to stop by the theater. He had gotten a ride in with one of Lizzy's brothers, and was asking Lizzy if she could drive him to the mechanic's to pick up his car so that he could take it to a funeral in the morning.

Oh, yeah, did I mention that Barry was a pastor? Well, he was, which made things a little more complicated for me when it came to trying to date his daughter.

Anyway, Lizzy couldn't take her dad to the mechanic's, because she was on the closing shift and wouldn't be getting out of work until 1:00 in the morning. So, me being the great person that I am (sarcasm is intended here, I did this entirely for selfish purposes), I offered to stay up late so I could take Barry to pick his car up at the mechanic after work that night, even though I was on the opening shift the next morning.

Barry accepted gratefully, and now I was excited because I had an opportunity to score some brownie points.

After work that night, I drove up the road to Barry's house to pick him up, and we set out on our way. As we were driving, we started to get to know each other a little better. He was telling me all about how he was a Boston Red Sox fan, which is something that we have in common. We talked about sports and music and all kinds of things for the first ten or fifteen minutes of the ride.

And then, out of the blue, Barry asked me the strangest, yet most important, question I would ever be asked in my life:

"Hey, by the way, where will you go when you die?"

I was totally caught off guard. I definitely didn't expect a question like this, nor did I know how to answer it. I sat silent for a few seconds, thinking about how I knew exactly where I was going, it was the same place everyone goes when they die: six feet deep. But I didn't want to say that to the pastor, so given that we were driving next to a field that was littered with hay bails, I ended up saying, "well, if we crashed right now and died, hopefully I'd end up in one of those hay bails. It'd be a softer landing."

His response? I quote: "No, you dingus, Heaven or Hell?"

I sighed. I knew this is what he meant, but I didn't know the answer so I didn't want to answer him. So, I just said, "Heaven, I hope."

Let's pause here for a second. Think about how terrifying my answer was. "Heaven, I hope." I had no certainty of my going to Heaven whatsoever, and the only other option presented to me was Hell. I was just living my entire life not knowing where I would spend my eternity. Would I spend it in eternal paradise? Or would I spend it in eternal suffering? I had no idea. How anxiety inducing is that - living while not knowing at all what your eternal standing is. Knowing that you could die at any moment, and you have absolutely no grasp on your eternity.

That is the situation that I found myself in at that moment. Barry asked me why I answered the way that I did, and I told him that I went to church almost every week, and that I did a lot of good things, and that I thought I did more good things than bad things. I started to explain some of those good things: I was an usher at church, I donated to charity sometimes, and I helped the old people at church carry things that were too heavy for them. I actually started to feel pretty good about myself as I was building my case for eternity.

But then, Barry hit me with another punch to the gut.

"I can tell you for certain, as it stands right now, you aren't going to Heaven."

So much for those brownie points I was trying to get.

"Why not?" I asked.

"Because," he explained, "if you were, you would know for sure."

I can know for sure? I thought. I immediately started wondering about how that could be possible. Was there a certain number of good things I needed to do? Was there a limited number of bad things I could do before I was kicked out of Heaven? Was there just one really big act of service I needed to perform in order to get to Heaven? Did I have to give a certain amount of money to my church?

"Nope," Barry replied when I asked him all of that. "You would know, because you would have asked Jesus, and He would have said 'Yes.'"

"Okay?" I replied skeptically. "I'm lost. All I have to do is ask Him?"

"That's right. All you have to do is ask Him. But, you're not asking Him to let you into Heaven, you're asking Him to forgive you for your sins. And then, when you're forgiven, God will let you into Heaven."

I still didn't fully understand, so Barry continued.

"Do you remember how Jesus died?"

"On a cross," I answered.

"Right. And do you know what sin is?"

"Bad things."

"It's more than that," said Barry. "It's when we go against God's commandments. Any time we go against God's commandments, that's called 'sin,' and the penalty for even one sin is eternal death and suffering in Hell. And the problem is, we're all sinners."

That made sense, but something was still off in my mind. "Then what's the point of Jesus if we're all going to Hell because we're all sinners?"

"That's the thing," Barry answered. "Even though we're all sinners, Jesus died on the cross to pay the penalty for our sins. So, when you ask Jesus to forgive you, He can, because He already paid the price for us. That's how I know I'm going to Heaven. I've told Jesus that I'm a sinner, and I've asked Him to forgive me, and He has. He's changed my whole life."

It was at this point that we pulled up to the mechanic's driveway.

"Well, it was great talking with you, Jack," Barry said as he stepped out of the car. "And here, I brought this in case you were interested. Maybe you can listen to it sometime." He handed me a CD. "And thanks again for the ride."

At this point, I had completely forgotten about Lizzy. (Sorry, Lizzy.) I wanted to know more about what Barry had just said. I put the CD in the car and started listening. As soon as I hit "play," I heard Barry's voice! It turns out that he recorded the CD. And no, thankfully, he wasn't singing. Instead, he was sharing his life's story, talking about his life before being forgiven by Jesus, the story that led him to ask for forgiveness, and what his life was like after he did.

I listened to it as I drove home. Barry was still driving in front of me, because he knew the way home and I didn't. And it was a good thing he was in front of me, because once we were half way home, he pulled over.

I pulled over behind him, and he got out of the car and started walking towards me. I rolled down my window.

"The car isn't fixed, it still has the same problem. We'll have to take it back."

So, I rolled my window back up and followed him back to the mechanic, still listening to his CD.

Once we got there, he got back into my car and mentioned something about his CD. He started to say, "If you ever decide to listen to it," but I cut him off.

"I actually did listen to it already, I started it on the way back and it finished as soon as we pulled into the driveway again."

Barry grinned. "So, what did you think?"

"I'm in," I replied.

"What do you mean?" he asked.

"I mean I'm in. I want to ask Jesus to forgive me."

"That's great!" he exclaimed. "Well then, let's pray!"

Why Asking Questions About Faith Matters

The question of "Where do we go when we die?" is not a new question. People from every generation, all the way back to ancient days, have asked about an afterlife. The Bible says that God "has put eternity into man's heart," meaning that we actually come pre-wired to to wonder about eternity (Ecclesiastes 3:11 ESV).

And God wants us to wonder about our eternities, but not because He thinks watching us struggle over something as important as this is some cruel game, but rather because He knows where we go, and wants to share the answer with us. The answer to the question of where we go when we die is that our informed choice about who Jesus is determines where we go: Heaven, or Hell.

At the end of this book, you'll get the opportunity to make this choice about Jesus for yourself, as I did that night in 2017. But, since you picked the book up, there's a good chance that you don't yet understand how important your decision about Jesus is. You may not even buy the whole "God" thing at all. Maybe you do believe in God, but you're wondering if everything the Bible says is true. Or maybe you're trying to make sense of several different religions, and you can't seem to nail down which one is true. It could be that you believe all of the religions are true, and that they're all just different paths that lead to the same place. Perhaps you don't even know how to decide what to believe, or you don't believe anything at all!

If you fall into any of those categories, or even if you fall into a category that I haven't mentioned, I'm so glad that you picked up this book. My hope is to provide you with scientific, historical, and logical evidence to prove to you that God is real, and that He cares deeply for each of us.

If you're going to make any decision in life, you should gather and evaluate the facts related to the decision before you make it, and the same is true when the decision is about faith. So, as you read this book, I want you to read it as if it's a record of a court case. I'll present you with evidence that points to a living, loving God, and I'll also bring up common questions relating to this evidence. Then, you get to be the jury, deciding for yourself what to do with the information. It's my hope and prayer that you'll come to the same conclusion about God that I did.

A Roadmap For This Book

I wrote this book to give you all of the evidence that Barry, along with several other people over the years, gave me to prove that Jesus can forgive sins. The book is divided into four sections:

The first section is dedicated to proving the existence of God, the reliability of the Bible, and the divinity and resurrection of Jesus.

In the second section, we'll talk about the overall point of Christianity, and we'll discuss why Christianity is so different from other religions.

The third section is dedicated to common questions about God, the Bible, and Jesus. In this section, we'll start to touch on some very personal issues, such as why there is suffering in the world and why Hell even exists.

In the final section, we'll reflect about what all of this information means for you, and what it looks like to follow Jesus, should you choose to do so.

Are you ready? I sure hope so, because we're about to dive in!

Jack Duga

Could It Be True?

Section 1: The Proof

"There's no way God is real. I've never seen him."
"The Bible is just a book of fairy tales."
"Jesus didn't rise from the dead, the disciples just stole the body."
Have you ever heard, said, or even thought any of these things? In this first section, we'll look at proof for the existence of God, the infallibility of the Bible, and the resurrection of Jesus.

Chapter 1: How Do We Know God Exists?

The man who is paralyzed from the neck down sees a homeless man walking around asking for change, and just wishes that he, too, could walk.

The homeless man sees a group of cyclists riding by and wishes he had a bike so that he could get a job.

At that same moment, one of the cyclists wishes that he had a car - even an old one like the one passing him - because it looks like it's going to rain, and being able to commute with a roof over his head would be so nice.

A woman drives by the cyclist in her rusty, old car, wishing she had a newer model, one that was reliable, so that she didn't have to get it fixed every other month.

Meanwhile, a man in a new sedan commutes to work, wishing he had an electric car because electricity is so much cheaper than gasoline.

He sees a woman in an electric car, who is wishing that she had a luxury car, because wouldn't it be nice to ride around in style?

She passes a woman driving a luxury car, but the luxury car owner only wishes she had a chauffeur, because the roads are too congested to be able to drive without stress.

Just as she wishes this, a limo streaks past her, the driver oblivious to the passenger in the back who, as she sips on her drink, is fuming at how long she has been sitting in traffic. She longs to fly in her own private plane, high above all the congestion with no other people to contend with.

As she wishes this, a man in a private jet flies overhead, looking down at the world below him, wishing that he ruled it all.

And 3000 years before this man in the jet was born, King Solomon, the richest king who ever lived, who had more gold, more musicians, more women, more luxuries, and more power than anyone else in the history of the world, wished he was dead, because he realized that life without God was completely meaningless.

So many people who experience life without God get caught up in the pursuit of fulfillment, only to realize that, even though they eventually achieve their goals, all of the money, power, fame, and relationships in the world will never be able to fill the God-sized hole in their lives. However, even those who realize that material possessions will never give them the fulfillment they seek *still* refuse to give God a chance to fill that void in their hearts. Why? In many cases, it's because they don't believe that God even exists.

Maybe you feel a void in your life, and no matter what you do to try and fill it, the void remains. After all, this void is huge. The truth is that it's God sized, and that means that only God can fill it. Maybe you don't believe in God, and if you do, you still don't believe that He can fill that void. If that sounds like you, I hope that this book will give you a few things to consider.

Let's start simply by laying a foundation. We'll begin looking at evidence to prove that God, as described in the Bible, does exist and, in fact, created the entire world and everything in it.

Why Evidence Matters

Imagine that one of your friends offers you $10,000,000 to jump off of a bridge, promising you that there's a net at the bottom waiting to catch you. Would you do it? If we're honest, there's probably a chance that you would think about it for a second, but if you were going to seriously consider jumping, you would ask for proof that a net was there first. (You should also ask your friend for proof that they really do have $10,000,000!)

Let's say your friend says that she has no proof of the net, nor does she have proof of the money. At that point, you would probably laugh at her and walk away from the bridge.

But now, let's say that your friend does have proof. She shows you the money; it's all there. She shows you where the net is tied. She shows you the signature from a safety team saying that the stunt is completely safe. And then, she says, "follow me," and jumps off the bridge. You see her land on the net, perfectly safe.

At this point, you may actually consider jumping off the bridge. You have all of the evidence you need to prove that the drop will be safe. The money would make your life immeasurably better. All you need to do is make the decision.

This is exactly what Christianity is like. Just like your friend in our example offered you $10,000,000 to make a decision, Christianity likewise offers something great, but what Christianity offers is far greater than $10,000,000. Christianity offers forgiveness for sins, a restored relationship with God, and eternal life in Heaven. And, just like your friend in our example gave you evidence to prove her claim, Christianity offers evidence to support its claim. But why is that evidence important?

Evidence for Christianity is important for the same reason it's important to get proof of the net before jumping off the bridge. If your life depends on whether or not that net is there, you should make sure it's there before trusting in it. You shouldn't just guess, or "go with your gut" when your life hangs in the balance. And, with Christianity (and really, any other religion), it's your *eternity* that hangs in the balance. Instead of using gut feelings alone to choose a religion to follow, or whether to follow one at all, you should gather the evidence!

"But," you might ask, "isn't religion about faith?" Yes, it is, but not blind faith. You see, it's true that we aren't going to know everything about God while we're still on Earth. There are plenty of questions we can't answer. But there are also plenty that we can. And putting our trust in God even when we don't know all of the answers is actually good faith. For example, we're never going to know the answer to the question, "How did God originate?" The Bible says that God always is, always was, and always will be. That's not really a concept that we, as humans, can wrap our minds around. However, that question going unanswered shouldn't stop us from believing in God, because we can certainly answer the far more important question, "Does God exist?" Knowing about God's origination doesn't affect the fact that He exists whatsoever.

It's important, though, to distinguish "faith" from "blind faith." Whereas faith is putting your trust in God even when you don't have all of the answers, blind faith is believing without any evidence, without any thinking, and without any grounding in truth. And whereas faith is encouraged biblically, blind faith is not.

Let's check out a few examples in the Bible that show how seeking evidence for the Christian faith is encouraged:

> 1 Peter 3:15 (NLT) - "Instead, you must worship Christ as Lord of your life. And if someone asks about your hope as a believer, *always be ready to explain it.*" (Emphasis mine). You can't explain anything you put blind faith in.

> Acts 17:2 (NLT) - "As was Paul's custom, he went to the synagogue service, and for three Sabbaths in a row he used the Scriptures to reason with the people." Why was Paul reasoning with the people there? Well, if you read the next few

verses, you'll see that he was comparing Jesus' life to prophecies made hundreds of years before in order to prove that He is the Messiah!

Isaiah 1:18a (NKJV) - "'Come now, and let us reason together,' says the Lord..." In this verse's context, we see that God has brought a legal case against the actions and attitudes of the people of Israel, and wants them to *logically* come to understand that they are sinners, and that God is offering them salvation from their sins.

Clearly, God wants us to see the evidence that He is who He says He is. After all, you wouldn't invite someone to investigate something that you were lying about! So, what do we have for evidence? Let's take a look at four pieces of evidence that all point to the existence of God.

1. **The Universe's Origin**

When I was a kid, I loved astronomy. Honestly, I still think it's really cool today. The idea that the universe is so vast that it's unobservable in its entirety is absolutely fascinating. Even more amazing is the fact that the universe is still expanding!

When scientists first observed the universe's expansion, they theorized it must have started from something tiny. And it makes sense – everything that grows starts small. Look at a tree: it begins as a tiny seed, grows into a sapling, and eventually towers dozens or even hundreds of feet tall. The same is true for you. You started as just a few cells, and now your body contains trillions!

Everything that grows naturally has a starting point. Knowing this, Georges Lemaître, a theoretical physicist, proposed in 1931 what remains the leading theory for the universe's origin: the Big Bang.[1] According to this idea, about 13.8 billion years ago, the universe exploded into existence from a super hot, dense particle – its "starting point."

But what caused the existence of that particle? That's a question science still can't answer. Some theorize the universe expands and contracts in cycles – but even then, something had to trigger the very first cycle. Without a cause, the Big Bang theory is incomplete. Everything that begins to exist must have a cause: babies don't appear out of nowhere, and dinner doesn't just pop onto the table without someone preparing it. The same logic must apply to the universe.

---

[1] American Museum of Natural History, "Georges Lemaître: Father of the Big Bang," American Museum of Natural History, accessed April 12, 2025, https://www.amnh.org/learn-teach/curriculum-collections/cosmic-horizons-book/georges-lemaitre-big-bang.

So what caused the universe? If time, space, and matter began at the Big Bang, whatever caused it must exist beyond time, space, and matter. And personally, I can only think of one thing that fits that description: God.

When you bring God into the equation, you finally have an explanation for creation that answers the question the Big Bang theory leaves open: Where did everything come from? God is the original Creator. Let's take a look at how the Bible describes the beginning:

> In the beginning, God created the heavens and the earth. The earth was without form and void, and darkness was over the face of the deep. And the Spirit of God was hovering over the face of the waters. And God said, "Let there be light," and there was light. (Genesis 1:1-3 ESV).

Does the Bible completely match the Big Bang theory? No - but it doesn't have to. The Big Bang is humanity's attempt to answer the question of the universe's origin, and it shows that even secular science recognizes that the universe had a beginning. However, the Big Bang theory itself is incomplete. It can trace the universe back to a tiny, dense point, but it can't explain how that point came to exist in the first place. As pastor and theologian John MacArthur puts it:

> We have only one account, as I said earlier, of the creation and that is the account of the creator. And he spoke in intelligent words. Far from the ridiculous notion that nobody times nothing equals everything. Far from the absurdity that chance, which is nothing, becomes the power of creation. Far from the irrational notion that time existed before there was creation. There's only one reasonable reality and that is that God is, and God is the creator.[2]

The Bible gives us the ultimate answer. God, who exists outside of time, space, and matter, created the universe by His sovereign will. Scientific theories may shift over time when faced with new observations, but God's Word remains has never had to change because of science. Rather, it has been proven time and again to offer a complete and trustworthy explanation for our origin.

---

[2] John MacArthur, "ChristoCreation: Christ as Creation's Eternal Word, Light of Man, and Source of Technological Wisdom," The Master's University News, accessed August 30, 2025, https://www.masters.edu/master_tmu_news/john-macarthur-christocreation-theotech-2021.

2. The Fine-Tuning of the Universe

I've played bass for most of my life. I love the deep sound and the rumbling feeling in my chest when I play those low notes. From rock bands like Rush, with their melodic bass lines, to jazz bands, where bass plays an important supporting role, I've always been a huge fan.

Something that makes playing the bass a little easier for me is my perfect pitch. If you play a note for me, I can tell you exactly what note it is. I don't need to have an instrument in hand to check, I can just tell you right on the spot. I know that my microwave buzzes to a "B." My wife's electric toothbrush plays a "C." And each of the keys on the piano I inherited from my grandmother are *almost* in tune. The keys are all in tune with each other, but they're all a little flat overall.

When I play this piano by myself, it sounds great! But if I have a friend playing the piano while I play the bass, the piano sounds *terrible*. Not because my friend doesn't know how to play piano, but because my piano is just a *little bit* out of tune. Likewise, when I try to play the piano along to a song through my speakers, everything sounds all wrong.

Isn't it interesting how, even though my piano is extremely close to being in tune, everything sounds all wrong when it's played? We're not talking about being three or four notes off here, just a fraction of one. Yet being off that fraction makes an extremely notable (and annoying) difference.

The same is true with the universe, and, most importantly, with the Earth. The conditions needed for a planet to be able to sustain human life are extremely specific. We need a planet that keeps its atmosphere within a specific temperature range, abundant liquid water, an atmosphere thick enough to shield us from harmful radiation, yet balanced enough to prevent a runaway greenhouse effect. We depend on just the right amount of solar energy, the correct balance of essential elements and nutrients, and a host of other finely tuned factors - and that's only scratching the surface.[3]

The chances of any one of these conditions being met on any given planet are extremely low. So low that this fact sparked the premise for the fictional movie, *Interstellar*.

In *Interstellar*, people were trying to find another habitable planet to live on. Each time they found a planet worth exploring, it met *almost* all of the requirements needed to sustain life, but it didn't meet *all* of them. Therefore, even if a planet only missed one requirement, it wasn't habitable.

---

[3] Lunar and Planetary Institute, Habitability Reference Table (Houston, TX: Lunar and Planetary Institute), accessed April 12, 2025, https://www.lpi.usra.edu/education/explore/our_place/hab_ref_table.pdf.

Just like the characters in *Interstellar*, we require a complex and finely tuned environment that isn't missing even one of the many necessary conditions to support life.

So what are the chances of all of these conditions being met on a single planet simultaneously? After all, we would need all of the conditions to be met if the planet is going to be considered habitable. If even one condition is just a little bit off, we wouldn't be able to survive.

And even if all of the conditions were right, does that mean life would automatically form? Absolutely not. Then what are the chances of life forming without an architect? Well, astrophysicist Fred Hoyle (who was *not* a Christian) once said that the odds of life forming by chance are about the same as a tornado sweeping through a junkyard and assembling a Boeing 747.[4]

I don't like those odds.

The data suggests that life did not happen by chance. And if it didn't happen by chance, then how did it happen? The most likely explanation is that there is a Creator. Let's explore this idea.

Take a look at the room around you. I'll bet you that everything you're looking at was created. The book in your hand was created (a fact that I can personally

---

[4] Fred Hoyle, The Intelligent Universe (London: Michael Joseph, 1983), 19.

attest to). The coffee mug on the table next to you. The couch you're sitting on. The lamp that's illuminating your book. None of it just materialized into the universe by chance. All of it was created by someone. This is common sense to us. Yet we look at the mountains, the trees, the oceans, the beach, the sky, and we think these were all randomly generated? I'm not buying it. Maybe mountains are randomly generated in video games such as Minecraft, but even then, Minecraft has a creator.

In summary, given the vast number of very specific conditions needed for a planet to be able to sustain life, it is extremely unlikely that any planet would be habitable to humans. Even if one were, there's an even smaller chance that life would form without an architect. Finally, as we discussed earlier, creation needs to have a creator. When we put all of these things together, we can safely conclude that there is a Creator, God, who created a planet that was so fine tuned that it was able to sustain life, and then the Creator created that life.

Let's read another excerpt from the creation story in the Bible to see what the Bible says about this:

> And God said, "Let the waters under the heavens be gathered together into one place, and let the dry land appear." And it was so. God called the dry land Earth, and the waters that were

gathered together he called Seas. And God saw that it was good. And God said, "Let the earth sprout vegetation, plants yielding seed, and fruit trees bearing fruit in which is their seed, each according to its kind, on the earth." And it was so... And God said, "Let there be lights in the expanse of the heavens to separate the day from the night. And let them be for signs and for seasons, and for days and years, and let them be lights in the expanse of the heavens to give light upon the earth." And it was so. And God made the two great lights—the greater light to rule the day and the lesser light to rule the night—and the stars... And God said, "Let the waters swarm with swarms of living creatures, and let birds fly above the earth across the expanse of the heavens."... And God said, "Let the earth bring forth living creatures according to their kinds—livestock and creeping things and beasts of the earth according to their kinds." And it was so... Then God said, "Let us make man in our image, after our likeness. And let them have dominion over the fish of the sea and over the birds of the heavens and over the livestock and over all the earth and over every creeping thing that creeps on the earth." So God created man in his own image, in the image of God he created him; male and female he created them. (Genesis 1:9–11, 14–16, 20, 24, 26–27, ESV).

Here, we see the rest of the creation story. It clearly lists God as the Creator of Earth and of life. Because the data shows that it would be nearly impossible for life to form on its own, and because logic shows that all creation must have a creator, the biblical account of creation stands strong, giving us one more piece of evidence that points to a God.

3. The Moral Evidence

When I was in college, I took a class in Anthropology. I signed up because I needed the credits, but I ended up really loving the class. I loved getting to learn about people from different walks of life. Learning about their different belief systems was fascinating to me, even though I wasn't a Christian yet myself. I wasn't the greatest student overall, yet I found myself up late each night researching different religions, from major religions with millions of followers, to small, tribal religions with only a few hundred followers.

Something that I noticed while studying all of these religions was that, in the vast majority of them, there are important similarities. Whether these religions worship one God, multiple gods, or no god at all, certain aspects of the religion are the same across the board.

The vast majority of religions are not okay with murder. They aren't okay with rape or adultery. They aren't okay with theft. They value benevolence. They value family. They value honesty.

Why, in many of these different religions, do our morals match so closely? Wouldn't you think that different religions who worship different gods would have different moral systems?

While it's true that there are people from every religion that go against the moral codes of their religions, I find it shocking how similar the written moral codes of each of these religions can be. Why is this the case?

To paraphrase detective J. Warner Wallace - if there is no God, everything is permissible - but we all know some things are not permissible. That tension only makes sense if a Moral Lawgiver exists.[5] This "Moral Lawgiver" would not just need to have existed since the rise of humans, he would have needed to create humans and put this "moral code" in our hearts. And, based on our evidence for a Creator, we can rightly assume that this Moral Lawgiver is God.

---

[5] J. Warner Wallace, God's Crime Scene: A Cold-Case Detective Examines the Evidence for a Divinely Created Universe (Colorado Springs: David C. Cook, 2015), 91.

To illustrate the point that there is a Moral Lawgiver, let's talk about a commonly despised individual - Adolf Hitler. Why is Hitler so commonly despised amongst people from all different faiths? Naturally, it's because of the atrocities he committed during his rule. But who decided that what Hitler did was atrocious? Some people may answer this question by saying, "No one has to define it, what Hitler did is just naturally bad." And, to this, I would agree, though I would also ask, "why is it *naturally* bad?"

You see, we need to get to the root of this question in order to fully answer it. Saying that something is "naturally bad" does not get us to the root. We can still dig deeper. And we do this by asking the question, "why?"

When we ask why something is "naturally bad," we get two options:

Option 1: All people decide for themselves what is good and what is bad, and we all unanimously just so happened to decide that what Hitler did was evil.

Option 2: There is a Moral Lawgiver who puts certain things in our hearts, telling us what is bad and what is good. Based on these moral laws, we know objectively that what Hitler did was evil.

Personally, I don't believe that so many people coming from so many different religions would unanimously agree on something unless there was a

Moral Lawgiver behind it. Yet, in Hitler's case, we have people from all religions who agree that Hitler's thoughts and actions were atrocious. Take a look at these examples from several prominent religious figures:

1. Lutheran Pastor Deitrich Bonhoeffer clearly detested the Nazi regime.[6]
2. Rabbi Abraham Joshua Heschel, a Jewish Rabbi and theologian, said, "There is no answer to Auschwitz. To try to answer is to commit a supreme blasphemy."[7]
3. Mahatma Gandhi, a Hindu leader and philosopher, wrote to Hitler that "your own writings and pronouncements and those of your friends and admirers leave no room for doubt that many of your acts are monstrous and unbecoming of human dignity."[8]

Here, we have three extremely different religions, yet all of them seem to have the same moral

---

[6] United States Holocaust Memorial Museum, Dietrich Bonhoeffer, Holocaust Encyclopedia, accessed August 30, 2025, https://encyclopedia.ushmm.org/content/en/article/dietrich-bonhoeffer.

[7] Abraham Joshua Heschel, quoted in Jewish Virtual Library, "Quotations on the Holocaust," accessed August 30, 2025, https://www.jewishvirtuallibrary.org/quotations-on-the-holocaust

[8] Mahatma Gandhi, Letter to Adolf Hitler, July 23, 1939, in Selected Letters of Mahatma Gandhi, accessed August 30, 2025, https://www.mkgandhi.org/letters/hitler_ltr1.php.

code in this regard. Though this is an extreme example, there are many other examples of this same phenomenon amongst many different religions, regarding a plethora of different issues.

It is clear that people all over the world, regardless of different religions, tend to hold many of the same moral codes. And if we all get to decide what is moral and what is immoral ourselves, the odds that all of these religions agree on so many things are extremely small. Why, then, do we all agree on these issues? The only explanation can be a Moral Lawgiver who puts these morals in our hearts. And that Moral Lawgiver is God, our Creator.

4. Personal Experience and Testimony

In the introduction of this book, I shared the story of how I came to know Jesus. As the story unfolded, you were probably interested in what was going to happen next. Maybe you were interested to see what kinds of crazy questions Barry would ask me. Maybe you were interested in seeing my response to those questions. And maybe you were just interested to see whether or not Lizzy and I would ever start dating. (If that was you, we are now happily married and have been for some time!) But, as you were reading, I'd bet that you believed each word I was writing about my story. And I'd bet that you believed it because I was telling you a personal story about something that really happened to me. I was telling you the truth as I experienced it.

If you were to hear my story and say, "No, Jack, that never happened to you," you would have absolutely no ground for your claim to stand on. You simply can't truthfully tell me that what I described never happened. The only one who could tell me that would be Barry, because he was there the whole time, but he recognizes my story as the truth.

This line of thinking brings us to the final piece of evidence we'll cover in this chapter for God's existence: people's personal experiences and testimonies.

I love the word "testimony" because it implies that the person with a testimony is a witness. In court cases, people who witnessed an event are called in to share their testimony with the court. These testimonies then serve as evidence throughout the rest of the case.

Christians also have testimonies, because we're also witnesses. We're witnesses of God's redemptive work in our lives. And we use our testimonies to tell others about how God has influenced our lives, in an effort to encourage others to invite God into their lives as well.

Even I was influenced by hearing someone's testimony. Do you remember the CD that Barry gave me? That CD was the story of how he came to Christ. It was his testimony. By sharing that CD with me, he served as a witness for the Lord. I quite simply could not tell him that what he was sharing was wrong, because it was something that he personally experienced.

Before I came to Christ, I regularly experienced terrible panic attacks. I wouldn't be able to leave the house, and sometimes wouldn't even be able to leave my bed. They would sometimes last for days, or even weeks.

After I came to Christ, they began to subside. The intensity of the panic attacks went down, and so did the frequency, to the point that I can't actually remember the last time I had an unprecedented panic attack. What changed? I didn't start taking any new medicine, I didn't start a new workout routine, I didn't move anywhere with cleaner air. The only difference was that I now followed Christ. In the Bible, the apostle Peter writes, "Give all your worries and cares to God, for he cares about you" (1 Peter 5:7 NLT). This is exactly what I did, and over time, I started to notice a big difference.

Can you tell me that it's just a coincidence that my anxiety started to go away as soon as I trusted in

Christ? Yes, you can. But if you did, I would ask, "Why did it happen immediately following my decision, and how did it happen at all if nothing else in my life changed?"

To me, here's what I know to be certain. I put my faith in the Lord. I gave Him my burdens, and He took them away from me, setting me free. No matter what anyone tells me, they will not be able to disprove my personal experience.

Common Questions

At this point, many people are a little more open to the idea that there's a God who created the universe, but there are still many questions that I haven't addressed thus far, and a lot of those questions are very popular. So, before we move on, I'd like to address some of those questions briefly in case any of them are floating around in your mind right now!

Many of these questions are about the Bible, Jesus, other religions, and suffering, all of which are very important, and will be given their own chapters in this book. The following is a list of questions specifically related to God:

Q: How can I believe in something that I can't see or measure?

A: This is a great question, and many people will answer it by saying something along the lines of, "You can't see air, yet you believe in that!" I, however, don't like that answer, even as a Christian myself. I can physically feel air when I'm riding in my car with the windows open. I can physically feel air filling my lungs with each breath. I can't physically feel God. I can, however, use deductive reasoning.. Because I can physically feel air, I have enough evidence to prove to myself that it exists. In other words, I believe in air because I've seen the evidence. So, when it comes to God, what evidence do we have that can prove He exists? I've just provided four pieces of evidence, and if you need more evidence, I would also encourage you to ask a Christian friend or family member who you trust why they believe in God. But, I believe in both air and in God because I have seen the evidence for both.

Q: If God is real, why doesn't He just show Himself?
A: He has! God has shown Himself to Moses through the burning bush, to the nation of Israel through the pillars of cloud and fire, as a whisper to Elijah, Isaiah saw God on His throne, and, most notably, Jesus is the image of the invisible God (Colossians 1:15). Many have seen God in manners such as these, but the vast majority of us have not. This is why Jesus says to doubting Thomas, "You believe because you have seen

me. Blessed are those who believe without seeing me" (John 20:29 NLT). We'll talk about why we can believe the Bible's account of these events in the next chapter.

Q: Isn't God just self-absorbed for wanting worship?
A: This is a very understandable question, because, let's face it; if any person claimed to be flawless, without sin, and also labeled themselves the "King of Kings," we would rightfully label them instead as "King of Ego." But what's important to know is that God doesn't actually need our worship. Worshiping God connects us to Him, and since God is the ultimate source of love, peace, joy, and a host of other things, we are the ones who really benefit from worshiping Him. Worship also becomes natural when we choose to follow the Lord. We worship what we love. So, when we love God, worship isn't something that we're forced to do. It is a natural result of how we feel.

Q: Doesn't science explain the universe now? Why do we need God?
A: I personally love this question, and the reason I love it is because science and God actually go hand-in-hand! Science explains *how* things work, but it doesn't explain *why* things exist in the first place. God explains why, and created orderly laws (science) for His creation to follow.

If you're still skeptical, don't worry! This is only the beginning of the journey. Throughout the rest of this book, we'll examine the answers to some important questions, such as:

1. How can we believe what the Bible says is true?
2. Who is Jesus, really?
3. What about other religions?
4. And one of the most asked questions: How can God be good if there's so much evil and suffering in the world?

As we move on to the next chapter, I want to invite you to do something bold: I want to invite you to pray. I know it may feel strange to you, but don't worry. You don't have to get down on your knees, it doesn't have to be long, you don't have to say "thee" or "thou" or "ye," and you can do it in your head. Pray to God, and ask Him for understanding as you continue learning more about Him through this book.

Chapter 2:
Why Trust the Bible?

Before I was a Christian, I thought that the Bible was nothing more than a common acronym: B.I.B.L.E., or, "Basic Instructions Before Leaving Earth." I thought it was nothing more than a rulebook. And, being a teenager, I decidedly didn't want any more rules in my life, so even though I owned a Bible, I never opened it.

Besides, I convinced myself, I go to church most Sundays anyway. If there was anything really important in there, the pastor would tell me! And if the pastor wasn't mentioning it, it couldn't be that important.

Here's the thing about the Bible. It definitely does contain "Basic Instructions Before Leaving Earth." One of its many purposes is to serve as a road map for our lives, teaching us how to make decisions and telling us where to turn. And the ultimate destination that this map leads to is Heaven.

But even more than a road map, the Bible is also a love letter from God Himself. You might think that sounds weird, but here's why we know it to be true: all of the different Bible stories that you may have learned growing up are just small pieces of the overall story of the Bible. And the overall story of the Bible is a true story about how God created us, loved us even when we rebelled against Him, and sacrificed His only Son for us so that we could be saved from the penalty of our rebellion. Isn't that amazing?

It's my hope that you'll come to understand both the love and the weight that the stories of the Bible carry. But before we can get into specifics about what the Bible says about God and Jesus and salvation and everything else you're probably wondering about, we need to talk about why we can believe that everything it says is true. (Yes, everything in the Bible is true, even the crazy miracles that it talks about!) For if we're going to balance our eternity on these basic instructions - this love letter from God - we should first know without a shadow of a doubt that it is true.

Think about it for a minute. If you're driving across the country, you're going to make sure that the map or GPS you're using is going to give you the right directions. Otherwise, who knows where you'll end up!

Well, if the Bible is a road map for how to get to Heaven, we should check to make sure it's really giving us the right directions, otherwise we'll end up being somewhere that we don't want to be.

Likewise, if you received a letter from a long lost relative, wouldn't you want to know it's really from them? And if it was, wouldn't you hang on every word? Well, if the Bible is a love letter from God Himself, we should definitely want to hang on every word of it!

Let's take a look at three pieces of evidence that prove the truth and the importance of the Bible.

1. The Bible's Remarkable Consistency

Imagine you hear rumors about something important happening in the world. Maybe it's something political, like an election; something economical, like a market crash; or something social that could spark a lot of arguments, like when you live in Boston and find out your new neighbor is a Yankees fan. Your local news normally takes sides on these sorts of things, so when you turn the news on, you aren't surprised about what they have to say. But, since this event is very important and you want to hear what the other side has to say as well, you turn on the opposing party's news station. To your amazement, they are saying the *exact same thing*.

You turn on a third, then a fourth, then a fifth news channel. All of them share the same facts. You then buy three different newspapers. The facts are the same. Each one has written their own story, each one tells the story in their own ways, yet the facts are the same across the board. This is what it is like reading the Bible.

The Bible isn't actually a book - it's a collection of books. Sixty-six, to be exact. These sixty-six books have over forty authors with wildly different backgrounds and personalities. They also all wrote at different times, with all of the books being written within a span of 1500 years. And they all share the same story about God. Isn't that remarkable? If you don't believe me, let's look at a few examples of how consistent the Bible really is.

1. The first example involves the overall theme of the Bible. Throughout the Bible, there is one theme that is consistently present: Reconciliation. In the book of Genesis, Moses writes that Adam and Eve sin against God, and God makes His first reference to a Savior who will save the world from sin and reconcile man with God (Genesis 3:15). About 700 years later, Isaiah prophesies a Savior who will save the world from its sin and reconcile man with God (Isaiah 52-53). In the book of Jonah, God sends a reluctant Jonah to the city of Nineveh to preach that repentance leads to

reconciliation (Jonah 1:2), and Nineveh repents and is reconciled with God (Jonah 3:6). In the Gospels (Matthew, Mark, Luke, and John), Jesus presents Himself as that Savior, offering reconciliation with God to whoever chooses to put their faith in Him.

2. The second example of the Bible's consistency involves specific prophecies that Jesus fulfilled. Let's take a look at some of the prophecies from the Old Testament and when they were written, and then we'll see how Jesus fulfilled each prophecy.

1. **Prophecy: Micah 5:2, written between 740-700 B.C.**
   But you, O Bethlehem Ephrathah, are only a small village among all the people of Judah. Yet a ruler of Israel will come from you, one whose origins are from the distant past.
   Fulfillment: Matthew 2:1-2, 1:1-17
   "Jesus was born in Bethlehem in Judea [which was the Roman pronunciation of Judah] during the reign of King Herod." In Matthew chapter 1, we see that His ancestry can be traced all the way back to Abraham, one of the patriarchs of the Jewish and Christian faiths.

2. **Prophecy: Psalm 78:2, written about 1000 B.C.**
   "I will open my mouth in parables; I will utter hidden things, things from of old."
   Fulfillment: Matthew 13:34-35
   "Jesus always used stories and illustrations like these when speaking to the crowds. In fact, he never spoke to them without using such parables. This fulfilled what God had spoken through the prophet: 'I will speak to you in parables. I will explain things hidden since the creation of the world.'"

3. **Prophecy: Psalm 41:9, written about 1000 B.C.**
   "Even my close friend, someone I trusted, one who shared my bread, has turned against me."
   Fulfillment: Matthew 26:47-50
   "And even as Jesus said this, Judas, one of the twelve disciples, arrived with a crowd of men armed with swords and clubs. They had been sent by the leading priests and elders of the people. The traitor Judas had given them a prearranged signal: 'You will know which one to arrest when I greet him with a kiss.' So Judas came

straight to Jesus. 'Greetings, Rabbi!' he exclaimed and gave him the kiss. 'My friend,' Jesus said, 'go ahead and do what you have come for...'"

4. **Prophecy: Psalm 22:18, written about 1000 B.C.**
   "They divide my garments among themselves and throw dice for my clothing."
   Fulfillment: Matthew 27:35
   "After they had nailed him to the cross, the soldiers gambled for his clothes by throwing dice."

5. **Prophecy: Numbers 21:8-9, written about 1400 B.C.**
   "And the Lord said to Moses, 'Make a fiery serpent and set it on a pole, and everyone who is bitten, when he sees it, shall live.' So Moses made a bronze serpent and set it on a pole. And if a serpent bit anyone, he would look at the bronze serpent and live."
   Fulfillment: John 3:14-15
   "And as Moses lifted up the serpent in the wilderness, so must the Son of Man be

lifted up, that whoever believes in him may have eternal life."

6. **Prophecy: Jonah 1:17, written about 760 B.C.**
   "And the Lord appointed a great fish to swallow up Jonah. And Jonah was in the belly of the fish three days and three nights."
   Fulfillment: Matthew 12:40
   "For just as Jonah was three days and three nights in the belly of the great fish, so will the Son of Man be three days and three nights in the heart of the earth."

7. **Prophecy: Psalm 22:1, written by King David about 1000 B.C.**
   "My God, my God, why have you forsaken me? Why are you so far from saving me, from the words of my groaning?"
   Fulfillment: Matthew 27:46
   "And about the ninth hour Jesus cried out with a loud voice, saying, 'Eli, Eli, lema sabachthani?' that is, "My God, my God, why have you forsaken me?"

8. **Prophecy: Isaiah 42:1, written between 739-681 B.C.**
   "Behold my servant, whom I uphold,my chosen, in whom my soul delights; I have put my Spirit upon him; he will bring forth justice to the nations."
   Fulfillment: Mark 1:10
   "And when he came up out of the water, immediately he saw the heavens being torn open and the Spirit descending on him like a dove."

These are only eight examples of prophecies that were fulfilled, but in total, there were over 300 prophecies made about the Messiah in the Old Testament, and Jesus fulfilled every single one of them.

Now, what is the probability that anyone would be able to fulfill all 300 prophecies? Well, just for fun, let's first look at the probability of someone fulfilling just eight of them. In his book "Science Speaks," Dr. Peter Stoner gives us a great illustration:

> Suppose that we take 10^17 silver dollars and lay them on the face of Texas. They will cover all of the state two feet deep. Now mark one of these silver dollars and stir the whole mass thoroughly. Blindfold a man and tell him that he can travel as

> far as he wishes, but he must pick up one silver dollar and say that this is the right one. What chance would he have of getting the right one? Just the same chance that the prophets would have had of writing these eight prophecies and having them all come true in any one man, from their day to the present time, providing they wrote using their own wisdom.[9]

And that's the chances of just *eight* of these 300 prophecies being fulfilled! That sounds like some pretty solid evidence to me.

3. Our third example of the Bible's consistency is that, even though the Bible was written over a period of 1500 years by forty different authors, the teachings are all unified. Some clear examples of this are the parallels between the Ten Commandments and the Sermon on the Mount.

The Ten Commandments, found in Exodus 20, were the basic rules that the nation of Israel was told by God to follow. Some of these commandments were instructions not to lie, murder, or commit adultery.

In Matthew 5, which takes place almost 1500 years later, Jesus preaches the most famous sermon

---

9 Peter W. Stoner, Science Speaks (Chicago: Moody Press, 1963), 106.

ever preached; the Sermon on the Mount. And Jesus pulled some of his material for that sermon from the Ten Commandments! He affirmed the teachings of the Ten Commandments, and then clarified them. For example, He said, "You have heard that our ancestors were told, 'You must not murder. If you commit murder, you are subject to judgment.' But I say, if you are even angry with someone, you are subject to judgment!" (Matthew 5:21-22a NLT).

Jesus affirms that it is a sin to murder, and then equates anger against someone with murdering them. He does this same thing when talking about adultery, divorce, vows, revenge, and loving your neighbors all in the same sermon. He affirms the Old Testament teachings and further clarifies them, showing us that the teachings in the Bible are unified and consistent.

We've seen three pieces of evidence for the Bible's remarkable consistency. Even so, couldn't people have made edits in the past 2000 years to ensure that it was consistent? Couldn't people have changed what was in the Bible over time to push their own agenda? Those are great questions, and I think that the answer will surprise you. Let's look at our second piece of evidence proving the truth of the Bible.

2. The Infallibility of the Bible

The question of whether or not we can trust today's Bible was honestly a huge stumbling block for me before I became a Christian. I didn't believe that the Bible could be completely historically accurate, because I thought that what we have today was a copy of a copy of a copy of a copy of a copy. There just had to be mistakes in there!

Additionally, I questioned why there are so many different versions of the Bible. Even in this book, you've seen me quote different versions. There's the King James Version, which most people know of because of its use of Old English. Then there's the New King James Version, the New Living Translation, the New International Version, the English Standard Version, the American Standard Version, the Message, and on and on and on. How are there so many different versions of the Bible? How can they all be direct translations?

Finally, I questioned whether the Bible was telling the truth about everything, or whether there were fictional stories included to teach us lessons. I mean, you have guys walking on water and turning water into wine and rising from the dead. That's all some pretty cool stuff, but you have to admit that it sounds like a fairy tale - not like something that actually happened.

If believing everything in the Bible is a stumbling block for you, as it was for me, I want to share with you what I learned about the Bible in hopes that it will help you too. But before we dive into that, first, we need to talk about how Christians view the Bible.

How do Christians View the Bible?

Christians believe that the Bible is inerrant. "Inerrant" simply means that when language, context, and audience are correctly taken into account, the original message that was given is without error. When Christians read the Bible, we work to understand it within these parameters and are able to read everything it says as truth. Now, of course, there are certain things in the Bible that we know to be sarcasm.

For example, in 1 Kings, the prophet Elijah and the prophets of Baal were having a competition to see which god was real - the God of Israel, or Baal. The prophets of Baal were trying to get Baal's attention, and Elijah mocked them, saying, "You'll have to shout louder!... Surely he is a god! Perhaps he is daydreaming, or is relieving himself. Or maybe he is away on a trip, or is asleep and needs to be awakened!" (1 Kings 18:27b NLT).

Now, of course, we know that Elijah is not speaking literally here. When he says "Surely [Baal] is a god," he is saying it sarcastically. And we know this because Elijah then explains Baal's silence by saying that he's probably just using his heavenly toilet.

Additionally, in the Sermon on the Mount, Jesus uses hyperbole to make a point. He says, "If your right eye causes you to sin, tear it out and throw it away. For it is better that you lose one of your members than that your whole body be thrown into hell" (Matthew 5:29 ESV).

Jesus here is using hyperbole to emphasize how serious sin is. Of course, it would be better to lose one body part on earth instead of going through Hell for eternity, but Jesus is not literally commanding people to gouge out their eyes if they look at someone lustfully. If that were the case, every single Christian would have no eyes. We know that this wasn't Jesus' literal teaching because, in the rest of the New Testament, there are precisely zero examples of eye gouging. Yet, Jesus continues to clearly teach on the seriousness of sin.

While there are some examples of sarcasm and hyperbole in the Bible, Christians believe that all of the events that happen truly took place as described. We believe that Jesus and Peter really did walk on water, and that Jesus turned water into wine. We believe that Jesus rose from the dead. And, in believing these things, we also are confident in the transmission and translation of the Bible. Why do we believe this? Well, we believe it because of how the Bible was written!

How the English Bible was Written

The original Bible, as we've talked about, was not written all at one time, nor was it written by one author. Additionally, it wasn't written in one language. The Old Testament was originally written in Hebrew and Aramaic, and the New Testament was written in Greek. We had to translate it to get an English version.

The thing is, many people believe that the Bible we have today is a copy of a copy of a copy, so on and so on. But the reality is that it's not. The Bible that we have today is a direct translation based on the best and oldest manuscripts of the text that we have today.

Okay, maybe that statement didn't "wow" you. It's still a copy after all! But, consider the fact that there are over 5,800 copies of the original New Testament writings, and over 10,000 copies of the original Old Testament writings! (Compare this to Plato's writings, which are considered extremely historically accurate, yet have just over 200 copies!)

Each of these original manuscripts has been compared with the others in order to verify the accuracy of the information. In the end, there actually were some mistakes! Some texts had a misspelled word here or there, and others accidentally used the wrong punctuation. But overall, there were no errors relating to content. If, right now, you're thinking, "But Jack, there are still mistakes! So the Bible can't be inerrant," let me illustrate it for you.

Imagine you're back in high school, and you're in detention. Your teacher has you write the sentence "I will not punch my friends" 10,000 times.

I will not punch my friends.
I will not punch my friends.
I will not punch my friends.
I will not punch my friends.
I wlil not punch my friends.
I will not punch my friends.
l will not punch my friends.
I will not punch my friends.

Did you catch the mistake? If you didn't, go back and find it. I'll give you a hint, it's a spelling error. Now let me ask you this: even with the spelling error, were you still able to understand what the line said? Of course you were! You were especially able to understand it given the many copies of the same line. Ultimately, this mistake was not a content mistake, it was a simple spelling error. (And to further prove to you that these mistakes are unimportant, there was actually a second mistake here - one of the uppercase "I's" is actually a lowercase "L".) These are the only mistakes found in any of the thousands of copies of the original biblical manuscripts.

If you still don't want to take my word for it, let's look at what some non-Christian historians have to say about the Bible's historical reliability!

1. William Albright, an American archaeologist, wrote, "Discovery after discovery has established the accuracy of innumerable details of the Bible as a source of history."[10]
2. Michael Grant, a British historian who studied ancient Rome, wrote, "If we apply to the New Testament, as we should, the same sort of criteria as we should apply to other ancient writings containing historical material, we can no more reject Jesus' existence than we can reject the existence of a mass of pagan personages whose reality as historical figures is never questioned."[11]

---

[10] William F. Albright, The Archaeology of Palestine (Harmondsworth, Middlesex: Penguin Books, 1960), 128.

[11] Michael Grant, Jesus: An Historian's Review of the Gospels (New York: Macmillan, 1977), 199–200.

3. Sir William Ramsay, a British archaeologist, wrote, "I began with a mind unfavorable to [the history of the New Testament]... but more recently I found myself often brought in contact with the book of Acts as an authority for the topography, antiquities, and society of Asia Minor. It was gradually borne in upon me that in various details the narrative showed marvellous truth."[12]

Even though these scholars hadn't put their faith in Jesus at the time of their research, they believe based on the evidence that the original writings and copies of the Bible are, at the very least, historically accurate. So, seeing as we still have a great number of very old and well preserved manuscripts from thousands of years ago, we were able to translate them directly into English, keeping the historical reliability of the text.

But what about all of the different English translations, like the King James and New Living translations? Well, these are still direct translations, the only difference is in the vernacular. In the 1600s, when

[12] Sir William Mitchell Ramsay, St. Paul the Traveller and the Roman Citizen, Chapter I ("The Acts of the Apostles: Trustworthiness"), in St. Paul the Traveller and the Roman Citizen (London: Hodder and Stoughton, 1904), 7–8, as accessed via Christian Classics Ethereal Library, https://www.ccel.org/ccel/ramsay/paul_roman/paul_roman.iv.html.

the King James translation was originally published, they regularly used words like "dost," "thou," and "brethren." Now, we say words like "do," "you," and "brother." Additionally, some of these translations may not use the direct translation of a word, but may define it instead. For example, instead of saying "Jesse begat David," many translations will say, "Jesse was the father of David." This helps the Bible to be more accessible to people today, while still completely preserving the accuracy of what was written.

All this information about accurate translations is great, but how do we know that the events depicted in the Bible actually happened?

3. The Archaeological Evidence

There is quite a bit of archaeological evidence that supports the historical records found in the Bible. These discoveries help us to confirm some things that were once unverifiable historically.

One such discovery was the Tel Dan Stele. The Tel Dan Stele is a stone discovered in Northern Israel in 1993, which bears an inscription that mentions the "House of David." The reason that this discovery is so significant is that there previously was very little physical evidence directly linking the David of the Bible to an actual historical figure.

Additionally, we know exactly where the biblical city of Jericho is. In the Bible, Jericho was in the land of Canaan (part of the land that God once promised that Abraham's descendants would inhabit). Once the Israelites were led out of their slavery in Egypt, they embarked on a conquest to claim this land. One of the cities that they reclaimed was Jericho, a city with massive fortifications. In the book of Joshua, God tore down the walls of Jericho, leaving it open for the Israelites to conquer. Archaeological findings confirm that the fortifications of Jericho fell about the same time that the Bible claims God tore them down.

An example from the New Testament is the Pool of Siloam. In Jesus' time this pool in Jerusalem was used for ceremonial washing and purification. According to the Bible, Jesus healed a blind man at this pool. And in 2004, archaeologists uncovered this pool, providing us with a more tangible connection to this event described in the Bible.

Another New Testament example is the Pilate Stone. Pontius Pilate, the Roman governor who handed Jesus over to be crucified, didn't really do anything else of note in his life. He was a bit of an underwhelming governor, and as a result, there is not a lot of archaeological evidence that links directly to him. Yet in 1961, the Pilate Stone was discovered, which, like the Tel Dan Stele was for David, is a stone with inscriptions that mention Pontius Pilate, giving us tangible evidence of his involvement in the Roman government during Jesus' day.

Finally, we have the Cyrus Cylinder, which was discovered in Iraq in 1879. The Cyrus Cylinder details several events involving Cyrus the Great, including when he allowed the Jews to return to their homeland to rebuild the Temple of God, thus ending the exile.

What Does This All Mean?

Thanks to the Bible's remarkable consistency, a thorough understanding of how the Bible was written, and all of the archaeological evidence, we have a basis on which we can trust the Bible historically.

Within the text of the Bible, God repeatedly describes events to an audience that, from their perspective, will take place in the future. We - being able to look back from our perspective - see with confidence that those events historically took place as described long after they were originally written down. This gives us great reason to trust the Bible as the inspired Word of God.

The Bible's consistency suggests a single Author inspiring each person as they wrote. Knowing how the Bible was written helps us to understand what we're reading today and make sense of anything perceived as an "error," and the archaeological discoveries being made simply serve as additional proof of the Bible's trustworthiness.

Knowing all of this is great, but the Bible isn't only meant to appeal to our intellect as a historical document, it's also supposed to speak to our hearts. So, as we continue throughout this book, I invite you to give reading the Bible a try. I think you'll come to learn, as I did, that the Bible is much more than a book of basic instructions before leaving Earth.

When you first open up your Bible, I recommend starting with one of the four Gospels: Matthew, Mark, Luke, or John. Each of these books is an account of the life, death, and resurrection of Jesus. You'll learn a lot about Jesus through reading these books, and they'll be perfect to read alongside our next chapter, which is also all about Jesus! We'll learn who Jesus is and also prove the greatest miracle He ever performed - the Resurrection.

Chapter 3: Who is Jesus, Really?

I don't really like baking, because I'm not much good at it. Every time I try to bake something, whether it be bread, muffins, or cookies, something is always wrong when it comes out of the oven. The bread didn't rise. The muffins, instead of having a nice puffy top, are concave. The cookies are flat and burnt. Why does this always happen?

Well, I've been known to forget certain key ingredients and steps when I bake. The bread didn't rise because I didn't activate the yeast. The muffins were concave because I didn't put in any baking soda. The cookies were flat because...well, I still haven't figured out why.

If we forget a key ingredient when we're baking, we may get a dessert that really tastes more like a rock.

Something will be wrong, so the dessert won't be complete. Believe it or not, Christianity is very similar to baking in this sense. You see, there's a secret ingredient to Christianity and, without it, Christianity would just fall apart - even more so than my cookies.

So what is this secret ingredient to Christianity? The secret ingredient is the resurrection of Jesus.

Listen, I get it. You don't believe that Jesus rose from the dead. Honestly, I can't blame you. It seems pretty far-fetched, after all. You mean to tell me that a guy who died the worst kind of death in human history came back to life and was perfectly fine just a few days later? Personally - even though I called myself a Christian for years - I, too, found the resurrection pretty hard to believe. I don't expect you to believe it either - at least not yet.

Up through this point, we've proved the existence of God, and we've talked about how the Bible is, at the very least, a historically accurate book that was inspired by God. But, when we look at what's written in the Bible, there is a LOT about the resurrection of Jesus. And that puts us at a bit of a crossroads.

On one hand, we don't believe in the resurrection of Jesus because resurrection is humanly and physically impossible. Yet on the other hand, we've proven the existence of God and the reliability of the

Bible, and both God and the Bible affirm the resurrection. So what should we believe?

We'll get into three very important topics throughout this chapter. We'll look at proof that Jesus was a real person, we'll look at what He said about Himself, and then we'll look at evidence for the resurrection. But before we look at any of these things, we need to understand why the resurrection is so important to Christianity.

To start, let's take a look at what the apostle Paul writes. Paul was someone who came to faith in Christ *after* the resurrection. Before he came to Christ, Paul actually persecuted Christians to the point of death. One day, however, he experienced Jesus himself (you can read about that in the book of Acts), and after that moment, he dedicated his life to telling others about Jesus. In a letter he wrote to a church in the city of Corinth, he wrote this:

> And if Christ has not been raised, then all our preaching is useless, and your faith is useless. And we apostles would all be lying about God—for we have said that God raised Christ from the grave. But that can't be true if there is no resurrection of the dead. And if there is no resurrection of the dead, then Christ has not been raised. And if Christ has not been raised,

> then your faith is useless and you are still guilty of your sins. In that case, all who have died believing in Christ are lost! And if our hope in Christ is only for this life, we are more to be pitied than anyone in the world. (1 Corinthians 15:14-19 NLT)

So what is Paul saying here? He's saying that Christianity itself hinges on the resurrection! The core message of Christianity is that we are all sinners, meaning that we've all rebelled against God. The penalty for sin is death. But God, in His love for us, sent us Jesus, His only Son, to save us from the penalty our sins deserve. And Jesus did this by doing two things. First, He died on the cross, taking upon Himself the punishment for our sins. Second, He rose from the dead, and in doing so, He defeated death. He proved that He was more powerful than death itself. With this also came the proof that He has the power to forgive our sins.

Paul is saying that If Jesus *didn't* rise from the dead, then He doesn't have the power to forgive our sins He claims to have. And if He can't forgive us for our sins, then our faith is useless because we're still guilty. Therefore, Paul explains, if the resurrection didn't happen Christians should be pitied more than anyone in the world.

As you can see, Christianity hinges on the resurrection. The resurrection is the main ingredient of Christianity. Without the resurrection, you have a concave muffin of a religion. Everything Christians do, whether it be reading the Bible, praying, going to church, singing worship music, is all just a bunch of nonsense if the resurrection didn't happen. But if the resurrection did happen, then that means Jesus *does* have the power to forgive us for our sins.

So, as we move on and learn about how we can prove that the resurrection did happen, I want to challenge you. As you read through this chapter, read it as if you're a historian looking for evidence. You don't need to make a decision as to what you'll do with the evidence yet. But I do want you to consider this question: Can we realistically prove that the resurrection happened? I believe that as you read through this chapter, like me, you will find that even though you might not believe in the resurrection right away, the evidence for it is overwhelmingly powerful.

So, let's dive into the proof. If we're going to prove that the resurrection happened, we'll need to answer a really important question first.

1. Was Jesus a Real Historical Figure?

In order to believe in the resurrection, we first need to believe that Jesus was a real person. Many people have opinions about Jesus; some think he was real, some think he wasn't. Some think that the stories about Jesus are mere fairy tales designed to teach us good morals. But what's important is that we don't make any decisions based on our opinions. Our decisions should be made on facts, and facts alone.

When I put my faith in Jesus, I had no doubt in my mind that Jesus was real. I had seen the facts! I would never dedicate my entire life to something that I wasn't able to prove, and I'm not expecting you to either. Before you make any kind of decision about Jesus, let's forget about our opinions and focus on the facts about Him.

The first fact we'll focus on is simply that Jesus was indeed a real person. We have plenty of Christian sources that agree that Jesus was a real person, but that's to be expected. (I mean, Christians worship the guy, so of course we'll say he's real!) Now that we view the Bible as a historically accurate document, it becomes an extremely powerful piece of evidence for Jesus' existence. But, we just spent an entire chapter talking about the accuracy of the Bible, so I would much rather focus on non-Christian sources for this chapter. Let's first take a look at Tacitus.

Tacitus (his full name was Publius Cornelius Tacitus), was a Roman senator, historian, and governor. His main focus was on Roman imperial history. And just as strong as his love was for Roman imperial history is his hatred of Christians. He was openly hostile towards Christians, both in his speech and in his writings. If there was anyone who would have benefitted from claiming that Jesus wasn't real, it was Tacitus.

Yet, in his work *Annals*, he writes, "Christus, from whom the name had its origin, suffered the extreme penalty during the reign of Tiberius at the hands of one of our procurators, Pontius Pilatus..."[13]

This was written around AD 116, just over 80 years after Jesus' death and resurrection. People were still alive who had seen Jesus crucified. Despite his hatred of Christians, Tacitus didn't even try to disprove the existence of Jesus, because he knew from first hand accounts that Jesus really did exist. For Tacitus to try to disprove Jesus' existence would have been like an English historian from 1800 trying to prove that George Washington, who lived until 1799, didn't exist.

[13] Tacitus, Annals 15.44, trans. Alfred John Church and William Jackson Brodribb (London: Macmillan, 1876).

Josephus gives us more evidence for Jesus' existence. Josephus was a Jewish priest, a Pharisee (a group of Jewish religious leaders who hated Jesus - they're the ones who convinced Pilate to crucify Jesus), military leader, and historian. Being a Pharisee, Josephus was decidedly against Christianity - the Pharisees not only hated Jesus when He was alive, but also tried to stamp out Christianity after He died.

Yet, in his work *Antiquities of the Jews*, he writes, "...so he [Ananus the high priest] convened the judges of the Sanhedrin and brought before them a man named James, the brother of Jesus who was called the Christ, and certain others."[14]

Here, Josephus, like Tacitus, doesn't even try to disprove the existence of Jesus. Josephus wrote these words in AD 93, even earlier than Tacitus wrote. It's clear from his writing that Josephus didn't *like* Jesus, we get that from how he writes "the brother of Jesus *who is called the Christ*" (emphasis mine). He's not calling Jesus the Christ himself, he's just reporting what others call Him. He's saying that James is "the brother of this guy Jesus, who people worship for some reason, saying he's some sort of savior." But just because Josephus didn't like Jesus doesn't mean he didn't believe He was real. He certainly believed that Jesus

[14] Flavius Josephus, Antiquities of the Jews 20.9.1, trans. William Whiston (Peabody, MA: Hendrickson Publishers, 1987).

existed, which we can clearly see by how he refers to James being His brother. He just didn't believe that Jesus was the Christ, or savior.

Still another account proving Jesus' existence comes from Pliny the Younger. Pliny the Younger was a Roman lawyer, author, and governor. In a letter to Emperor Trajan dated back to AD 112, he wrote, "They [the Christians] were in the habit of meeting on a certain fixed day before it was light, when they sang in alternate verses a hymn to Christ, as to a god..."[15]

He reported to the Emperor that the Christians were worshiping Jesus as if he were some sort of god. Again, he didn't like that people were worshiping Jesus, and he certainly didn't participate in the worship, but he was surprised that people were worshiping someone who he knew for a fact was killed on a cross.

All of these sources from non-Christians have two things in common. First, they hated Jesus and His followers. Second, even though they hated Him, they never even thought to deny His existence as a historical figure. They definitely denied His divinity, but they all confirmed that He did, in fact, exist.

Because of their evidence, we also can know without a shadow of a doubt that Jesus existed. But was Jesus divine? Let's take a look at what Jesus Himself

---

[15]Pliny the Younger, Letters 10.96, in The Letters of the Younger Pliny, trans. Betty Radice (London: Penguin Books, 1969).

said about that, and then, just for fun, let's try to disprove Him.

2. What Did Jesus Claim About Himself?

Let's say that, right now, I told you that I am God. (I'm not telling you that for real - it's just hypothetical. I am, in fact, not God.) But if I claimed to be God, you would have to think one of three things about me. C.S. Lewis famously listed out these three options in his book *Mere Christianity*. He told us that you would either need to believe that I was a liar, that I was a lunatic, or that I was Lord.[16] Now, if I told you that I was God, you could label me as both a liar and a lunatic. I am not God, and I would be crazy to think that I was. But, Jesus legitimately claimed that He is God, so let's take a look at His claims and see if He's a liar, a lunatic, or if He's really Lord!

First, Jesus claimed to be God. As He was talking to a group of nonbelievers, He said, "I tell you the truth, before Abraham was even born, I AM!" (John 8:58b NLT). Back in the Old Testament book of Exodus, Moses asked God what His name was, so that he could tell Pharaoh who sent him to free the people of Israel from their slavery to Egypt. God then revealed to Moses in Exodus 3:14 that "I AM WHO I AM." (Exodus

[16] C.S. Lewis, Mere Christianity (New York: HarperOne, 2001), 52.

3:14b NLT). So when Jesus says the words "I AM," He is directly referencing God in Exodus, which we can understand as a claim to be God.

Second, In John 10:30, Jesus says, "The Father and I are one." (John 10:30 NLT). "The Father" is another reference to God.

Finally, in Mark 14, right before Jesus was sentenced to death, the high priest asked Him if He really was the Messiah, the Son of God. "Jesus said, 'I AM. And you will see the Son of Man seated in the place of power at God's right hand and coming on the clouds of heaven'" (Mark 14:62 NLT). Notice the "I AM" statement in this verse too. This is another example of Jesus claiming to be God.

So, since Jesus is claiming to be God, let's analyze our options. Is He a liar, a lunatic, or is He really Lord?

You may be wondering why I'm not including a fourth option, that option being that Jesus was just a good moral teacher. Here's why. If Jesus was simply a good moral teacher, He would not have claimed to be God. If He did, He would have been a good moral teacher who was also a liar (which, when you think about it, isn't really possible), or a good moral teacher who was also absolutely crazy to think he was God (which, again, isn't really possible). Jesus would have been a *fantastic* moral teacher if He didn't claim to be

God, don't get me wrong! But, as we've just seen, He *did* claim to be God, so we have to rule out the option that He was simply a good moral teacher.

Now that we understand our three options, let's look into option one: Jesus is a liar. Assuming we believe the Bible is a historically accurate document, this theory can be debunked pretty easily. Jesus made many claims while He was on Earth, and He proved all of them to be true. Here are just a few of these claims and how they were fulfilled:

> **Claim:**
> In Luke 11:20, Jesus claimed to have power over demons: "But if I am casting out demons by the power of God, then the Kingdom of God has arrived among you" (Luke 11:20 NLT).
> **Fulfillment:**
> Jesus fulfilled this claim before He even made the claim in the first place. In Luke 8, Jesus casts out a group of demons from a man by commanding that they enter a group of pigs instead. In verse 33, we read that "Then the demons came out of the man and entered the pigs, and the entire herd plunged down the steep hillside into the lake and drowned" (Luke 8:33 NLT).

Claim:

In Mark chapter 4, Jesus claimed to have power over nature during a huge storm: "When Jesus woke up, he rebuked the wind and said to the waves, "Silence! Be still!" (Mark 4:39a NLT).

Fulfillment:

If Jesus didn't have power over nature, nothing would have happened. Yet, in the second half of verse 39, we see that "Suddenly the wind stopped, and there was a great calm" (Mark 4:39b NLT).

Claim:

In John chapter 11, Jesus claimed to have power over death after his friend Lazarus died. He told Martha, Lazarus' sister, that Lazarus would rise again. "Jesus told her, 'I am the resurrection and the life. Anyone who believes in me will live, even after dying'" (John 11:25 NLT).

Fulfillment:

Jesus proved that He has power over death by raising Lazarus from the dead. "Then Jesus shouted, 'Lazarus, come out!' And the dead man came out, his hands and feet bound in graveclothes, his face wrapped in a headcloth" (John 11:43-44a NLT).

Jesus made a lot of claims, but as He fulfilled all of them, we can't reasonably call Him a liar. But, could He be a lunatic?

To determine whether or not Jesus was a lunatic, we need to examine His character. Lunatics are often described as crazy, erratic, psychotic, unfocused, and out of their minds. Does Jesus' behavior match this description? I don't believe it did in the slightest.

Insane people don't talk the way Jesus talked. They don't think the way Jesus thought. If you read through the Gospels (Matthew, Mark, Luke, and John), you'll see that Jesus had one goal in mind: to give His life as a ransom for many - to give His life so that all of us could be forgiven for our sins. He never strayed from that goal. It was always on His mind, and He always talked about it to His disciples. A lunatic wouldn't be able to hold focus on that goal for the 33 years that Jesus did.

A lunatic also wouldn't heal the sick like Jesus did. A lunatic wouldn't be able to get people to actually listen to his teachings. And, most of all, a lunatic's life wouldn't be marked by kindness and mercy and compassion as Jesus' was. (Look at how He treated the woman at the well in John 4 and the prostitute who was about to be stoned in John 8 for two examples of His compassion). So, clearly, Jesus was not a lunatic.

This leaves us with one final option, and that option is that Jesus is telling the truth - He is Lord. What's the evidence for this? Well, for one, we can use the process of elimination to figure this out. We've proved that Jesus isn't just a great moral teacher, He isn't a liar, and He isn't a lunatic. These are the only options that can be reasonably considered aside from Him being Lord.

But if you want proof outside of the process of elimination for Jesus' Lordship, we can actually look at some of the same evidence that we used to prove that the Bible is historically accurate, consistent, and God-inspired.

Do you remember Dr. Stoner's illustration of the odds that eight of the prophecies about Jesus would be fulfilled? If not, go back to chapter two and take a look at it again. The odds were extremely low, to the point that they're basically impossible without some sort of divine intervention. All of these prophecies were about the Messiah - the Lord. And Jesus didn't just fulfill eight prophecies, He fulfilled 300. If the fulfillment of 300 prophecies isn't enough to convince you that Jesus is Lord, I don't know what will. The evidence is overwhelmingly strong.

So, we know that Jesus was a real person, and now, we know that Jesus rightfully claimed to be God. But we still haven't answered the question about Jesus' resurrection. Did that really happen? And if so, how do we know it's not just a made up story? How do we know the apostles didn't just steal His body from the grave, or create some other sort of cover story? These are all great questions, and it's really important that we answer them, because remember, Christianity hinges on the resurrection. So let's take a look.

3. Is There Evidence for the Resurrection?

It all boils down to this. If Christianity hinges on the resurrection, then everything Christians believe is dependent on there being enough evidence to prove that it really happened. And if you're going to believe in Jesus, then you need the evidence for the resurrection as well. But in order to believe in the resurrection, you first need to believe that Jesus really died on the cross.

There are several theories claiming that Jesus never died on the cross, and instead claim that Jesus survived the crucifixion, though He was wounded so badly that the Romans *thought* He was dead. These theories state that Jesus later regained consciousness in the tomb, or that He ascended into Heaven while still alive, and sent someone else into the tomb for three days instead. However, we read in John 19 that on the day Jesus was crucified:

> It was the day of preparation, and the Jewish leaders didn't want the bodies hanging there the next day, which was the Sabbath (and a very special Sabbath, because it was Passover week). So they asked Pilate to hasten their deaths by ordering that their legs be broken. Then their bodies could be taken down. So the soldiers came and broke the legs of the two men crucified with Jesus. But when they came to Jesus, they saw that he was already dead, so they didn't break his legs. One of the soldiers, however, pierced his side with a spear, and immediately blood and water flowed out. (John 19:31-34 NLT)

One of the reasons that crucifixions were so brutal is that they were always slow and painful deaths. This is because the lungs of the condemned were stretched to the inhale position, so in order to exhale, the person on the cross would need to push up on their ankles, which normally had nails driven through them. Each breath was agonizing, yet people could maintain this pain for many hours. Because of this, if the death needed to be quicker, the Roman soldiers would break the legs of the condemned, rendering them unable to push up on their ankles. Within minutes, they would die of asphyxiation.

This is exactly what the Roman guards were going to do to Jesus, yet before they did it, they realized He was already dead. However, these Romans knew that if Jesus was taken down from the cross and wasn't really dead, they would be killed in His place. So, they did something that would have killed Jesus even more quickly than breaking His legs - they rammed a spear up through his side. And then, the Bible says that "blood and water flowed out."

Blood flowing out of a spear wound makes sense, but what about the water? Well, this "water" was pericardial effusion (fluid around the heart) that is caused by hypervolemic shock, which occurs when the body has lost a significant amount of blood - which Jesus had as he was scourged before the crucifixion. And, as they were professional killers, the Romans knew that this pericardial effusion was proof that someone on the cross had already died. So, although they would have been killed if Jesus was taken down from the cross alive, they still confidently took Him down, because they knew without a doubt that Jesus was dead.

This is why William D. Edwards, a Professor of Pathology at Mayo Clinic, said that "modern medical interpretation of the historical evidence indicates that Jesus was dead when taken down from the cross."[17]

Based on this information, we can be assured that Jesus did die on the cross, and now, with that assurance, let's talk about the proof that He rose from the dead!

The Empty Tomb

The first piece of evidence that points towards the resurrection of Jesus is the empty tomb. Jesus died on the cross and then was buried in a tomb owned by Joseph of Arimithea. The Bible says that on the third day after being buried, however, Jesus rose from the dead, which would have meant that the tomb would be empty. But did that really happen?

Surprisingly, historians on both sides of the resurrection argument actually agree that Jesus' body wasn't there. But why? We see a historical account of the event in Matthew. Let's pick up right after the two women who discovered Jesus' tomb empty leave to tell the disciples:

---

[17] William D. Edwards, Wesley J. Gabel, and Floyd E. Hosmer, "On the Physical Death of Jesus Christ," Journal of the American Medical Association 255, no. 11 (1986): 1455, https://lehighvalleychurch.com/wp-content/uploads/2020/04/Medical-Account-of-the-Crucifixion-.pdf.

> As the women were on their way, some of the guards went into the city and told the leading priests what had happened. A meeting with the elders was called, and they decided to give the soldiers a large bribe. They told the soldiers, "You must say, 'Jesus' disciples came during the night while we were sleeping, and they stole his body.' If the governor hears about it, we'll stand up for you so you won't get in trouble." So the guards accepted the bribe and said what they were told to say. Their story spread widely among the Jews, and they still tell it today (Matthew 28:11-15 NLT).

Why is this important? Well, even Jesus' greatest enemies knew that the tomb was empty. They didn't argue that fact at all! Instead, they tried to create a cover story for it. If the tomb wasn't empty, they wouldn't have needed a cover story. They could have just gone into the tomb and looked at the body. But again, since there was no body there, they needed the cover story to explain what happened. So clearly, the tomb was empty, which points to a resurrection.

But just to cover all of our bases, let's play devil's advocate and talk about that cover story a bit more. How do we know that someone didn't just steal the body? Actually, there are several ways of proving this, as well, but let's take a look at my favorite piece of evidence.

Saul's Conversion

The second piece of evidence that points to the resurrection of Christ is Saul's conversion. Saul was the former name of the apostle Paul who we talked about earlier, and he was the *least* likely person to believe in the resurrection. His entire job was persecuting, arresting, and even killing Christians, and he loved it. What would make someone like this come to Christ?

Saul himself experienced the resurrected Jesus. In Acts 9:3, Saul was traveling to Damascus when a bright light shone around him and literally knocked him to the ground and blinded him. Verses 4-6 describe Jesus speaking to Saul. But couldn't that have been a hallucination? It's highly unlikely, because verse 7 says that "the men with Saul stood speechless, for they heard the sound of someone's voice but saw no one!" (Acts 9:7 NLT).

Then in verse 27, Barnabas confirms that while the men with Saul didn't physically see Jesus, Saul did. Take a look:

> Then Barnabas brought him to the apostles and told them how Saul had seen the Lord on the

way to Damascus and how the Lord had spoken to Saul. He also told them that Saul had preached boldly in the name of Jesus in Damascus (Acts 9:27a NLT).

We can see that Saul both saw AND heard the Lord. And remember, this Saul that saw Jesus is the same Saul whose job was stamping out Christianity entirely. It is highly unlikely that Saul, of all people, would say that Jesus rose from the dead, unless he experienced the risen Christ personally.

But in case you still aren't convinced that Saul wasn't simply hallucinating on that hot, long, road to Damascus, let's look at our next piece of evidence.

The 500

In 1 Corinthians 15:6, Paul states that Jesus appeared to over 500 people after the resurrection. In this letter, he tells people that most of these witnesses are still alive, and that if anyone doesn't believe in the resurrection, all they need to do is ask these witnesses. This is very powerful evidence, because logically, if Paul didn't truly believe that these people saw the resurrected Jesus, he never would have encouraged his audience to ask the 500 about Him.

There is a common argument made about this piece of evidence, which is that all of these people were hallucinating when they "saw Jesus." But, as Gary Habermas and Michael Licona wrote in their book *The Case for the Resurrection of Jesus*, "Hallucinations are private occurrences. They are not collective experiences. If one person has a hallucination, others cannot share it. It would be like several people all having the same dream at the same time—while awake. This has no basis in psychological research."[18] So now, aside from Paul, we have 500 eyewitnesses of the resurrected Jesus. If that's still not enough, let's take a look at one last piece of evidence.

The Martyrs

When trying to prove that the resurrection didn't happen, we also need to remember that most of the apostles suffered and died because they continued to preach about the resurrection. I don't know of a single person who would die in order to defend something that they knew was a lie. Yet, the apostles suffered and died to defend their faith in the resurrection. If the resurrection was made up, they would have admitted it while they were being tortured. After all, they would

[18] Gary R. Habermas and Michael R. Licona, The Case for the Resurrection of Jesus (Grand Rapids, MI: Kregel Publications, 2004), 111.

have had firsthand knowledge if any one of them had stolen Jesus' body. They had the opportunity to renounce their faith and live when faced with death, but they didn't. They continued to stand for the truth of the resurrection even unto death.

I would venture to guess that, if they thought that the resurrection was a lie, they would have admitted it when the torture began. I know that I wouldn't suffer being tortured for a lie - much less would I allow myself to be tortured to the point of death. Would you?

Many of us today are like Doubting Thomas. We say that we'll never believe unless we see Jesus physically. When Jesus let Thomas touch His wounds from the crucifixion, Thomas believed. "Then Jesus told him, 'You believe because you have seen me. Blessed are those who believe without seeing me'" (John 20:29 NLT). And it is my hope that, at this point, you believe, even if you have not seen Jesus physically.

At this point, we have evidence for the existence of God, the validity of the Bible, and the truth of the Resurrection. There are now a few questions that you're likely asking: What's the point? Why does any of this matter? What should I do now that I have this information? We'll answer these questions in the next section of this book.

Jack Duga

Section 2: The Point

Based on the proof, you now know that God is real, the Bible is accurate, and Jesus rose from the dead. That's all great, but what's the point? In this section, you'll see what Christianity is all about.

Chapter 4: What Is This All About?

Now that we have all of the evidence pointing to the existence of a Creator (God), proving the historical accuracy of the Bible, and validating the resurrection and divinity of Jesus, it's time to talk about what all of this is about. It's one thing to know that God exists on an intellectual level, but it's another thing entirely to put your faith in Him and devote your life to Him. Throughout the next two chapters, we'll talk about what it means to put our faith in Jesus, why we should do it, and how we know that Christianity is the truth.

We're operating under the assumption that you believe the evidence that was presented thus far. I think that the evidence is overwhelming, and I hope that you've realized that as well. But, if you don't yet believe it, I encourage you to continue to seek more evidence. If you picked up this book, it's likely that you don't want to blindly put your faith in something - or someone. And as we've touched on, you shouldn't operate on a blind faith. Faith in Christianity isn't about shutting your eyes and hoping for the best. The Bible says that "Faith shows the reality of what we hope for; it is the evidence of things we cannot see" (Hebrews 11:1 NLT). Even though we can't physically see God, faith is being absolutely sure of His existence.

Imagine you're at a church on Sunday, and the pastor starts praying. "Heavenly Father," he starts, "if you're out there somewhere, please make yourself known to us." That doesn't sound very faithful, does it? Christians don't just believe that God is "out there somewhere." We *know* that He's there, we know that His Word (the Bible) is the ultimate truth (whether or not we like it), and we know that Jesus rose from the dead.

So, if you're not at the point that you believe those three things yet, I want to encourage you not to operate on a blind faith. Instead, keep looking at the evidence. Read the first few chapters again, or even do some further research yourself. Because, starting now, we're going to move away from giving proof, and we'll start talking about what we should do in light of the proof that we now have. We'll do this by talking about three main questions:

1. What does it mean to put my faith in Jesus?
2. Why do I need to make Jesus my Lord and Savior?
3. What changes when I say "Yes"?

In order to answer these questions, we need to start at the beginning. In the Book of Genesis, the first book of the Bible, we see an account of the creation. The creation started on the first day, when God said, "Let there be light" (Genesis 1:3b ESV). God created the light, and He saw that it was good. Over the course of the next five days, God created everything else in the world. And each time He created something, He saw that it was good.

When the Bible says "good," it actually means "perfect." There was nothing wrong with it at all. Back in the first couple of chapters of Genesis, everything was perfect. The only thing that wasn't perfect was that Adam, the first human, was alone. So, God made Eve as a companion for Adam. Adam and Eve lived in the Garden of Eden along with God - a picture of perfection on Earth.

Immediately after the account of creation, we see an account of what we call "the fall." God had previously told Adam and Eve that they could eat the fruit from whatever tree they wanted - except for the Tree of the Knowledge of Good and Evil. God said that the day they ate the fruit from that tree, they would surely die. And it was soon after this that Satan showed up. (You've probably heard of him - if not, he's commonly known as the devil. More on him in chapter 6.)

Satan tricked Eve into eating the forbidden fruit, and Adam just stood there watching. This was mankind's first sin. Sin is actually an archery term. It means to "miss the mark," or to "fail to achieve a desired outcome." The mark set in Genesis was that Adam and Eve would follow one simple rule. Don't eat the forbidden fruit. They were in charge of the whole Earth - God had put everything under their authority so long as they didn't eat that fruit. But, they sinned. They missed the mark. They broke God's commandment. Therefore, their relationship with God was broken, and they handed over all of their authority on Earth to Satan, inviting the curse of sin upon themselves and upon the Earth.

This curse of sin is the root of all of our problems today. Because of sin, the world is no longer perfect. It's under Satan's authority right now, and it will be until Jesus comes back to Earth for a second time to take that authority back.

And, with Satan ruling the Earth right now, he's trying his hardest to lead people away from God. Do you remember how God said that the day Adam and

Eve ate the forbidden fruit, they would surely die? Well, when they ate that fruit, they invited death into the world. And since we're all descendants of Adam and Eve, our relationship with God is broken and we're afflicted by the curse of their sin as well. And this is why we not only die a physical death, it's also why, without Jesus, we die a spiritual death. The term "spiritual death" is used by Christians to refer to our state of separation from God. If we linger in our spiritual death until the time of our physical death, then we go to a place called Hell, which is a place where God eternally pours out His wrath on sin.

This all sounds pretty awful, right? I agree. Every Christian and Non-Christian alike would agree. The reality is that we're all in a terrible mess that started just because some people decided to disobey God. But here's the thing - it wasn't only Adam and Eve who sinned, it's all of us. We've all missed the mark at some point. The mark is perfection, and none of us are perfect. So what does that mean for us?

Unfortunately, that means that we're destined to have to pay the penalty for our sins.

But what if I told you that this all sounds awful to God as well?

In the Bible, we see that God created us in His own image. And He loves us like parents love their child. Actually, He loves us much more than that; God doesn't just love us, He *is* love! (See 1 John 4). And would a loving God sentence the entire human race to eternal punishment and death? No, of course not! God is just, and the penalty will have to be paid, but in God's love for us, He made a way for us to escape the penalty. This is where Jesus comes in.

We know that Jesus is the Son of God. He *is* God. And when God saw that people had sinned, He enacted His plan. He knew that the penalty for sin was death, and there was no getting around that penalty. So He sent Jesus, His only Son, to pay the penalty for us.

Jesus was born of the virgin Mary, and because He was conceived by the Holy Spirit, He wasn't subject to the curse of sin that the rest of us were. He lived a perfect life, never sinning. Not even once. And the only way He could do this was because He literally is God. But, as we talked about in our last chapter, Jesus died on the cross, even though He did nothing deserving of death. *But why?* Why would Jesus die when He didn't have to?

Well, it turns out that He died a substitutionary death. He died in place of someone else. He died in place of a sinner, so that that sinner could go free instead. And that sinner is *you.* That sinner is *me.* He died for *all of mankind,* so that our relationship with

God could be restored, and so that we could be freed from the penalty of our sins.

The most famous words in the Bible come from the book of John: "For God so loved the world that he gave his one and only Son, that whoever believes in him shall not perish but have eternal life. For God did not send his Son into the world to condemn the world, but to save the world through him" (John 3:16-17 NIV84).

To paraphrase: God so loved you and me and everyone else in this world, that He sent His only Son down to die on the cross in our place, so that when we put our faith in Him, we won't have to suffer the penalty of our sins, but we can be forgiven. God didn't send Jesus down to judge us - He sent Jesus down to save us.

The truth is that we're all sinners in need of a savior. And Jesus is offering to be that savior. So how do we accept this salvation? In the book of Romans, the apostle Paul explains, saying, "If you openly declare that Jesus is Lord and believe in your heart that God raised him from the dead, you will be saved" (Romans 10:9 NLT). That's all there is to it.

It seems easy, right? There's no trick here - it is as easy as it sounds! The hardest part about it is also making Him your Lord; in other words, making Him your King and following Him with your life instead of following your own desires. Many people will ask Jesus to be their savior, but will never choose to follow Him as Lord. Jesus needs to also be your Lord if you want Him to be your savior. But when you make Jesus your Lord by repenting of your sins, and you believe in your heart that He is the Son of God, He forgives you and also becomes your savior! And at that moment, He also promises you eternity in Heaven. This is what Christianity is all about. It's all about repairing our broken relationship with God that was caused by sin, and we do this by making Jesus our Lord and our savior.

Let's backtrack for a minute and talk about that word "repent." That word has a pretty negative connotation these days, so I want to explain it to you in its proper context. When you repent from something, you turn away from it. That's all it means. And when we choose to follow Jesus, we need to repent from, or turn away from, our sins. The apostle Paul writes in Romans, "Don't copy the behavior and customs of this world, but let God transform you into a new person by changing the way you think" (Romans 12:2a NLT). The behavior and customs of this world refer to sin. So, we're not giving into our sinful natures, we're turning away from them.

When we turn away from something, there's always going to be something that we turn towards. Picture physically turning around. When you turn around, whatever is in front of you ends up being behind you, and whatever was behind you is now in front of you. When you turn away from your sins, your sins start in front of you, and they end up behind you. And Jesus, who was behind you, ends up in front of you.

Does this mean that you'll become perfect and never sin again once you repent and put your faith in Jesus? I wish, but unfortunately not. Even when we trust in Jesus, we're still people, and we still have the same temptations that we had beforehand. We'll still have the temptation to judge others, to lie, to lust, to hate, to steal, to go against God's commandments. And honestly, we'll still give into temptation at times. The difference between the Christian and the non-Christian is that the Christian has been forgiven, whereas the non-Christian has not.

As Christians, over time, we will learn to better handle these temptations. When we become Christians, the Bible says that we're filled with the Holy Spirit, which is part of the Trinity. The Holy Spirit is God Himself, just as Jesus is God. And through the Holy Spirit, we're sanctified, meaning that, over time, as we focus more on growing in our faith in Jesus, we will start to become more like Him. We'll start to do the things that are pleasing to Him, and will sin less frequently. But sanctification isn't instant, it's a process, and it takes time. There will always be times when we fail. And when we do, we just need to ask the Lord for forgiveness. Many people will question if they'll lose their salvation each time they sin. Let me assure you that you will not. As long as you're focused on loving Jesus and becoming more like Him, then when you fall, He'll lift you up. That's called "Grace." And Jesus has an infinite amount of grace for us. Jesus as Lord wants us to follow Him because He knows the path that leads to Heaven, and Jesus the Savior has an infinite amount of grace for us when we occasionally stray off of that path.

We've talked about quite a bit here, so let's summarize the answers to those three questions from earlier:

1. **What does it mean to put my trust in Jesus?**

Putting your trust in Jesus means asking Him to forgive you for your sins, and trusting that He will. It's believing that He is the Son of God who has the power to defeat sin, and believing that He died on the cross to pay your sin penalty so that you don't have to pay it yourself.

2. Why do I need to make Jesus my Lord and Savior?

Hopefully, no one is forcing you to make Jesus your Lord and Savior. I get a bad taste in my mouth whenever someone tries to force me to do something. Technically, you don't *need* to put your trust in Him, it's your choice whether you do or not. But, putting your trust in Him is the only way to escape the penalty of sin, so if you want to be forgiven for your sins, then you actually do need to put your faith in Him and make Him your Lord for that to happen.

3. What happens when I say "Yes"?

When you make Jesus your Lord and Savior, several things happen! You are immediately forgiven for all of your sins. You stop trying to earn your way into Heaven because you are granted the promise of eternity in Heaven when your time on Earth comes to an end. You are filled with the Holy Spirit. You begin to become more like Jesus. You are adopted into God's family.

Before we bring this chapter to a close, I want to talk about something that I see all too frequently. When told about how they can receive salvation, many people reject it because Christianity supports a worldview that is much different than our society's worldview.

It's true that there are many things in the Bible that are listed as sin that our society today wouldn't agree are sinful. I won't go into examples here, though I'm sure that you can think of a few examples yourself. Maybe the examples you're thinking of have even prevented you from putting your faith in Jesus.

Many people don't become Christians because they stand for something that Christianity stands against, or they stand against something that Christianity is for. But why should we hang our eternities on such small things as these? Even issues that seem big here on earth are small when it comes to eternity. We're on Earth for an average of about 75-80 years. But eternity is forever. We're all going to face eternity one way or another - why would we dedicate our short lives on Earth to something that can't give us eternity?

You don't actually have to like everything about Christianity to become a Christian. You don't have to agree with all of the Biblical values to become a Christian. It's not about values, it's not about political or social stances. It's simply about trusting in Jesus. If you've been considering becoming a Christian, but you don't agree with Christianity's values, I want to encourage you to tell God exactly what you don't agree with, but then tell Him that you trust Him anyway. Over time, God will reveal to you why things are the way that they are, and we'll need to trust that He knows best (He did create the entire universe, after all). But, please, don't let something as small as an Earthly value get in the way of your eternity.

Some of you may be ready right now to put your faith in Jesus. If you'd like to do that, don't wait! Jesus is ready to receive you with open arms right now! Just tell Him that you'd like to follow Him. The prayer doesn't have to be pretty, just tell Him what's in your heart. You can do that in whatever way you choose, or if you'd like, you can skip ahead to the conclusion of this book to see a sample prayer that you can pray. If you decide to give your life to Jesus, congratulations! And if you're not ready yet, don't worry! You'll have another chance at the end of this book, and in reality, Jesus' offer to trust in Him is open for as long as you're still alive. If you still have some hangups, we'll address those throughout the rest of the book!

Chapter 5: What About Other Religions?

When I was searching for the truth about God, one of my big questions was about which religion was true. I had gone to church for my whole life, yet I believed that there were multiple ways to get to Heaven. I thought that you could choose between any number of religions, and that as long as you were practicing a religion, you would end up in Heaven in the end.

One day, I was talking to a friend about my theory (which I've since realized is quite mainstream), and they responded with a story of sorts, which I'll paraphrase for you.

Imagine you're on the Titanic. It's the adventure of a lifetime, a journey on the biggest ship ever built. Suddenly, you feel a shake and hear a deep rumble. You pause what you're doing to listen to what's going on. And you hear screams. People are shouting, saying that the ship is sinking. You felt the rumble, so you believe them. You start making your way to a life raft.

Once you find a life raft, someone tells you that there's a hole in the raft. Then, they point to another life raft a few dozen yards away - a fully functional one - and tell you that there's enough room on it for everyone on the boat. You can't see the hole in your current raft, so you have to choose whether or not to believe this stranger. If you decide to change rafts, you're worried that it won't actually be big enough for everyone and will fill up before you get to it. If you choose to get on this raft, you will be guaranteed a spot, yet what if that hole is really there?

Scenario One: You choose to stay with your raft. You climb into it and the Titanic sinks. As you're floating on the raft, you quickly see water starting to pour in. Your raft is sinking right along with the boat. Looking out on the horizon, you see the other raft filled with people, including the person who told you that there was room on it for you. You also notice an empty seat next to him. As you sink to your death, you think about how that person had just done the most loving thing they could have done for you; they had tried to get you to choose the good raft, yet you didn't listen to them.

Scenario Two: You choose to switch rafts, momentarily giving up the peace of mind that you would have if you'd stayed with your own raft. However, once you board the big raft, you regain your peace of mind as you float away to safety. With mixed emotions, you watch the other raft sink, realizing that the most loving thing that stranger could have done for you was to tell you about the hole, and you're so grateful that you listened.

When I heard that story, its implication became clear to me. This person was telling me that Christianity is the big life raft without holes that has room for everyone. But he was also saying that all of the other religions, though they may give the illusion of safety, are the life rafts with holes in them.

In this chapter, we'll answer three questions about Christianity and other religions:

1. Aren't all religions basically the same?
2. How can Christianity claim to be the true religion?
3. What about good people in other religions?

1. Aren't all religions basically the same?

To someone who doesn't play sports, all sports look pretty much the same. This is the case for my wife. She can become an expert at anything she sets her mind to, but not once in her life has she shown the slightest interest in setting her mind on sports. To her, you can summarize just about any major sport with one line: "You win when you get the ball to the other side more than the other team does." Even though my wife says this jokingly, let's think about it for a minute.

In a rudimentary way, this statement may seem true. But when you do think about it a little bit, there are different "scoring conditions" in each sport, even when the ball gets to the other side. With football, all you need to do is get the ball to the other side. You score when the ball enters the End Zone. But with soccer, you need to get the ball to the other side, then get it in the goal. And you can only use your feet. With basketball, you get the ball to the other side, but there's a very small basket you need to get the ball into that's 10 feet up. And you *can't* use your feet in this sport. In baseball, you have to use a bat to get the ball to the other side, but whether or not you get a point depends on whether or not you can run the bases before the ball gets back.

If I was playing basketball and started kicking the ball like it was a soccer ball, I would probably get ejected from the game. Likewise, if I brought a baseball bat onto the soccer field, I'd get a red card before the game even started. And if I tried to dribble a baseball, I would surely be letting my team down, and my parents as well.

To someone who doesn't play sports, it's possible that they all look the same if you don't know anything about them, but it's clear that they are all very different as soon as you start diving into even the most basic of rules. This is the same with religion. Many people who have never studied religion will claim that all religions are the same, and that they all get you to the same place. But when you do start studying them, you realize that's not the case. In fact, some of these major religions are aiming for completely different end results!

For the remainder of this section, let's take a look at five different religions: Christianity, Judaism, Islam, Buddhism, and Hinduism. We won't do an in-depth study on each religion, but I do want you to have an understanding of what each religion believes. Additionally, we're looking at key doctrines here. In every case, there will be different sects, denominations, or individuals that believe slightly different things, so we'll be sticking closest to the key doctrines taught in the holy books of each religion. We'll start with a recap of Christianity.

Christianity:

The ultimate goal of Christianity is to restore our relationship with God. This relationship was broken because of sin, and that sin condemns us to death. However, Jesus Christ, the Son of God, died on the cross as payment for our sin, and when we put our faith in Him by repenting of our sins and asking for His forgiveness, we receive eternal life in Heaven.

Judaism:

The ultimate goal of Judaism is to live faithfully in a covenant relationship with God. Judaism, the oldest of the Abrahamic religions, is rooted in God's covenant with Israel and obedience to the Law of Moses, which was given by God as the way to maintain that relationship. However, Christians believe that when Jesus died on the cross, the way of salvation shifted from obedience to the Law to faith in Jesus Christ. Unlike Christians, Jews do not believe that Jesus is the Son of God, and therefore continue to see obedience to the Law, rather than faith in Jesus, as the path to eternal life in Heaven.

Islam:

The ultimate goal of Islam is to enter into paradise in the life after death. In fact, Muslims worship Allah, which is simply the Arabic word for "God." They see themselves as worshiping the same God as Jews and Christians, as Islam is also rooted in the faith of Abraham, though Muslims believe the Quran corrects misunderstandings in earlier scriptures. They honor Jesus (Isa) as a prophet and Messiah, but not as the Son of God. Muslims believe that Muhammad is the final and most significant prophet, because he received the revelation recorded in the Quran. They believe salvation and entry into paradise depend ultimately on Allah's mercy, given to those who have faith and live righteously.

Buddhism:

The ultimate goal of Buddhism differs significantly from what we've seen so far. Buddhists are not trying to receive eternal life in paradise. Instead, they seek Nirvana, the cessation of suffering and rebirth. Buddhism does not center on worshiping a creator God as Christianity, Judaism, and Islam do; rather, Buddhists believe that all beings suffer because they are caught in the cycle of birth and rebirth, fueled by the "three poisons" of desire, aversion, and delusion. The Buddha was a man who attained enlightenment and taught others the way to reach it. To escape the cycle of birth and rebirth, one must extinguish these poisons by following the Noble Eightfold Path, which involves cultivating wisdom, living ethically, and practicing meditation. Through this path, a person may attain Nirvana. Nirvana is not a physical place, but a liberated state of being.

Hinduism:

The ultimate goal of Hinduism is to achieve Moksha, which, like Nirvana in Buddhism, is freedom from the cycle of rebirth (samsara). Hindus believe in Brahman, the ultimate reality, and the many deities they worship are often understood as different manifestations or aspects of Brahman. Upon attaining Moksha, Hindus believe a person can experience union with, or realization of, Brahman. There are several paths to this liberation, including devotion to a deity (bhakti yoga), knowledge of the self and of Brahman (jnana yoga), selfless action (karma yoga), and meditative discipline (raja yoga).

Though the descriptions of these religions are extremely short, we can already see that they aren't the same, and they aren't trying to be. Saying that two religions are the same because they both teach their followers to "do good" is like saying that baseball and football are the same because they both "have a ball." Ultimately, there are so many differences between baseball and football that even my wife would laugh at you for making the claim that they're the same.

Likewise, there are so many differences between all of these religions, not least the fact that even though they all teach people to "do good deeds," each one teaches us to do so for entirely different reasons.

Knowing now that all of these religions are different, we're faced with a big question: how can Christianity claim to be the true religion?

2. **How can Christianity claim to be the true religion?**

Do you remember the lifeboat that we talked about earlier? If you're on the Titanic and it's sinking, you need to make sure you find a lifeboat. And you need to make sure that the one that you choose isn't going to have any holes in it. Similarly, if we're talking about religion, we're talking about our eternities. Some claim that you only have one chance at life, others claim that you have many. All of them claim that salvation is gained through different manners. If you're ever on a sinking ship in real life, one of the things you're likely hoping is that your lifeboat is sound, and the other is that the religion you chose is the one that will really save you. And luckily, we know which religion that is.

Throughout this book, we've learned that God is real, that the Bible is historically accurate, that it was given by God, and that Jesus really did rise from the dead. The proof shows that Christianity is true. But does that mean that the other religions aren't true?

In short, yes. Let me illustrate it to you.

When I was 15 years old, I got my first car. It was a gray 1999 Isuzu Rodeo. My dad is a mechanic, and someone had brought it to his shop. The owner of the Rodeo wasn't looking to fix it though, he was actually there to fix the truck that was towing it to the junkyard. My dad asked him what he was doing with the Rodeo, and when he had said he was taking it to the junkyard, Dad said, "how much are you junking it for?"

"$300."

"Can you come back at lunch time? I can have $300 in cash for you, and you can leave the car here."

So, my dad bought the Rodeo for $300. I was super excited when he brought it home. Did I care about the fact that it didn't run? Nope. How about the fact that it had a huge crack all the way down the windshield? Nope. What about the ceiling that was yellowed from cigarette smoke, and the awful smell that came along with it? Okay, I did care a little bit about that. But I didn't care enough to let it deter me from making it drivable.

Over the course of the next year, my dad got the car running, and I cleaned it up...a little bit. It didn't run well, and the smoke smell still lingered a bit, but it was good enough that I could drive it as long as I didn't go above 70.

When I got my license at 16, I could drive the car, but I didn't really know how to get anywhere yet. So, I needed to use MapQuest. For those of you who were born after the turn of the century, MapQuest was what Christopher Columbus used to map out his trip to India. Okay, all jokes aside, you basically just put your destination into a website and MapQuest would give you a list of directions to print out. If followed correctly, they would get you to your destination. (Columbus didn't follow his MapQuest directions correctly, which is why he ended up in America rather than India).

Each time I went to drive somewhere new, I would hop on MapQuest and type in my destination. Then, MapQuest would give me the directions. If I followed the directions, I would get there, and if I didn't, then I wouldn't.

But what would happen if I typed in the wrong address in the first place? Well, if I typed in "100 Main Street" instead of "100 Main Road," I would never get to my destination. I would get somewhere that I didn't want to go. And with the state of my Isuzu Rodeo, I would need to pray really hard that it wouldn't die before I could figure out what the correct directions were.

So what does MapQuest have to do with religion? Well, too many people think of different religions as different directions that all lead you to the same place. But, as we learned, many of these religions aren't even trying to bring you to the same place. And even out of all of the religions that are trying to lead you to the right place, only one of them is giving you the right directions. If you follow the directions of the other religions, then even though they claim they're taking you to the right place, in the end, you won't get there. You'll be like Christopher Columbus, who landed on the entirely wrong continent because he didn't know that he was on the wrong route.

In the Bible, Jesus and His disciples discussed the way to get to Heaven. Take a look at their conversation, where Jesus gives them both the destination (Heaven, or, "my Father's home"), and the way to get there.

> "Don't let your hearts be troubled. Trust in God, and trust also in me. There is more than enough room in my Father's home. If this were not so, would I have told you that I am going to prepare a place for you? When everything is ready, I will come and get you, so that you will always be with me where I am. And you know the way to where I am going."

> "No, we don't know, Lord," Thomas said. "We have no idea where you are going, so how can we know the way?"
> Jesus told him, "I am the way, the truth, and the life. No one can come to the Father except through me."(John 14:1-6 NLT).

Here, Jesus tells His disciples, and us along with them, that our destination is His Father's home, which we know as Heaven. He also tells us the way to get there - through him. And as we have already learned, what Jesus means by this is that the only way to Heaven is to repent from our sins and to put our faith in Him for forgiveness.

We need to remember that these words are from the person that we have proven to be the Son of God, and they were written in the book that we have proven to be completely accurate and inspired by God. This means that when Jesus says that He is the way, and that no one can come to the Father except through Him, that there is only one life boat that is free of holes. And that life boat is Christianity.

Oftentimes, people will ask me if it's arrogant to say that Christianity is the only way to God. Won't that statement offend other people? And the truth is that, yes, it will offend other people, but no, it is not arrogant in the slightest. It's actually loving. It will offend people because it will challenge their current beliefs and their way of thinking, but it is loving because sharing the Gospel gives someone else the opportunity to know the One True God. When I share the Gospel, I'm sharing it in hopes *not* that people will conform to a certain set of behaviors, but rather in hopes that they will use the information to ask Jesus for forgiveness so that they can enjoy eternal life.

Think of it this way. Several years ago, our world came to a crashing halt due to the COVID-19 pandemic. Everyone was in quarantine, national and international travel was suspended, and state borders were closed. The virus would wait two weeks before displaying its first symptoms, so by the time you started coughing, the virus was already well established inside of you. COVID-19 stripped away the senses of taste and smell from thousands upon thousands of people. It left others with life changing symptoms that are still present in its victims even though the virus itself is not. And if that wasn't bad enough, it caused millions of deaths. Consider this: If a doctor had found a cure to that disease, would it have been arrogant to share it? Not at all! The most loving thing that the doctor could have done would have been to share that cure with everyone as urgently as possible.

The reality is that the virus of sin is inside everyone, and its after-effects are much worse than those of COVID-19. The virus called sin has eternal after-effects. As Christians, we know the cure for this virus: the gospel - the good news that Jesus is offering us forgiveness for our sins. And it's our job to share the gospel with people. It's not our job to force people to accept it, but it is our job to let people know where the cure lies. The most loving thing that we can do as Christians is to share the reality that Jesus is offering everyone eternal life when they put their faith in Him. Sure, it will offend some, but again, it's not our job to force it. It's our job to share it.

But what about those who don't accept it?

3. What about good people in other religions?

This is a very good question, and admittedly it is one of the hardest for Christians to answer. The reason it's hard to answer isn't because of how intellectually complex it is - it's actually quite simple. I think that it's hard for most people to answer because we all know that there are some great people in every religion, and there are also great people who don't belong to any religion at all.

The truth about Christianity is that true Christians don't believe they're better than anyone else. We're not better at all, we're just forgiven. As Christians, we mess up all the time. We're just willing to admit our mistakes, and not just to other people, but to God Himself. And because we've come to God with our sins, He's forgiven us through Jesus. We will continue to sin occasionally, though hopefully not as much, and there's a lot of good that we'll do as well. But we aren't better than anyone else. Being "better" isn't what gets us to Heaven. If it was, Christianity would have no point. We could just pick any other religion. Being *forgiven* is what gets us to Heaven. So to answer the question about good people from other religions, ultimately, good people don't go to Heaven. Forgiven people do.

This is actually quite great news when you really think about it. Anyone, from any religion, regardless of their background, can choose to ask Jesus for forgiveness. Regardless of your past, Jesus will meet you where you are. He will forgive you. And when He does, you will also be granted eternal life in Heaven. Christianity is the only religion that doesn't require you to earn your way to your destination. It's the only religion that teaches that God loves you so much that He purchased freedom for you.

Good people in other religions are actually carrying quite a burden. They're doing all of these good works to try to earn their way to salvation, yet they will never know if they were good enough to make it. With Christianity, they can be assured of their salvation, and then all of their good works are done with extra passion, because they're being done as a way to praise God for saving them and for lifting their burden.

The message of Christianity may offend some people, and in fact, it often does. In reality, anything that challenges someone's beliefs is likely to ruffle them. But it's important to remember that, as Christians, we're sharing the cure to sin because it's the most loving thing to do. The ship will eventually sink and there's only one functional lifeboat. It's a matter of life or death to make sure everyone gets on it. And thankfully, the lifeboat of Christianity doesn't have a capacity limit.

Section 3: The Problems

At this point, you understand the main point of Christianity and you have the proof that points to Christianity as the one true religion. However, you may not be ready to make a decision about Christianity yet. There might be one or two questions that you still just can't wrap your mind around. In this section, we'll address the most common of these questions.

Chapter 6: Why Would a Good God Send People To Hell?

In the summer of 2024, there was a record number of wildfires all across Canada, especially in Quebec. The fires were intense, and produced so much smoke that it visibly affected the air all the way down to my home in Connecticut. Millions of people living in the fire's path were evacuated from their homes, leaving all of their possessions - everything that they've worked for their entire lives, the places where they made so many memories - to escape the danger of the fires. In some cases, the fires didn't end up reaching the homes, but in many cases, they burned them to the ground.

The majority of people who were warned evacuated and were brought to safety. But what if someone didn't want to leave their home? "The fire will never reach me," they might have said. "I'm not moving an inch."

Some people chose not to evacuate, even though they were warned about it, and even though they had authorities and loved ones begging them to relocate. If the fire ended up coming to their house and they stayed, it was ultimately their choice to stay in the line of danger.

This situation is, unfortunately, what many people put themselves in eternally as well. God warns us about an eternal danger called Hell, yet some people choose not to evacuate to safety; they instead stay right where they are. And it's the reality that some people do go to Hell that leads us to ask the question, "If God is good, *why* do people go to Hell?" If we're going to fully understand the answer, then first, we need a little bit of background information on Hell.

1. The Background

It's important to know why Hell exists in the first place in order to answer the overall question of our chapter. The answer to this question is interesting, because the vast majority of people have either an incorrect or incomplete understanding of Hell. Ultimately, Hell was not created for people who are in a relationship with God. The Bible talks about a "God [who is] our Savior, who wants everyone to be saved and to understand the truth" (1 Timothy 2:3b-4 NLT). God wants everyone to be in a relationship with Him, meaning that He doesn't desire that *anyone* should need to spend eternity in Hell. This leads to the question of why Hell even exists in the first place. Actually, Hell was created as a place of eternal suffering for Satan, who rebelled against God, and for anyone who chooses to join Satan in this rebellion.

Yes, you heard right. Satan doesn't rule Hell, as is the popular belief. Hell was created as a place for him to suffer. You see, in the Bible, there are lots of references to a battle between God and Satan. You can see these in several books, such as Revelation, Ezekiel, and Isaiah. They can be tricky to put together, so I'll put them all together for you.

Satan once was one of the archangels, a high ranking angel who had splendor and a close proximity to God. Unfortunately, he was not content with simply being close to God - he wanted to *become* God. So, he took matters into his own hands and tried to take God's place. The angels that were under Satan fought alongside him, though to no avail. He was cast out of Heaven. This is when he was given the name "Satan," which comes from a Hebrew word meaning "adversary," "accuser," and "opponent." The angels that followed Satan were cast out of Heaven as well, and are now called demons.

Throughout time, God has given His message to certain people called prophets, and these prophets both spoke God's message to the people and also wrote them down. By reading the messages that these prophets wrote (which we can find in the Bible), we see that Satan's ultimate destination is Hell. There are several prophecies about how Jesus will defeat Satan and the demons once and for all in the battle of Armageddon, at which point, they will all be thrown into the "lake of fire and sulfur" (Revelation 20:10 ESV). But this hasn't happened yet. Currently, Satan is still under the delusion that he can beat God, and is trying to amass an even greater force to fight with him. And that force that he's amassing doesn't just include demons, it also includes people.

Fortunately, if we read the Bible, we know that God's side is going to win this battle. We also know that Heaven was created for everyone who is in a proper relationship with God, and that it's God's will for everyone to be in this kind of relationship with Him. Because of this, we also know that Hell was only created for those whom, like Satan and the demons, *choose* to remain in an adversarial relationship with God.

2. The Choice

I mentioned that Satan is trying to recruit people for his "team" in the battle against God. And likewise, God is recruiting for His team. But do you have to choose a team? Or can you be like Switzerland, who is known for its feat of remaining militarily neutral for centuries?

In the battle of God versus Satan, there is no Switzerland. The reason is because either God or Satan is going to have complete control and authority over the world once the battle is over. Switzerland is its own country; it owns its own land, and it runs its own government and military. It has the authority to decide whether or not it wants to join in any foreign conflict. But, let's say that someone invaded Switzerland. It would no longer have the luxury of remaining neutral. It would have to take a side, and it's extremely likely that it would choose to defend itself from the invader.

The battle of God versus Satan isn't a foreign battle. It's a battle that involves us directly. But rather than being a battle for land, it's a battle over our hearts and our eternities. God and Satan both want our hearts. God created us in His own image, and Satan is the invader. He invaded our hearts way back at the beginning of creation when he tricked Adam and Eve into eating the forbidden fruit. Now, it's up to us to determine whether we want to allow Satan to reside in our hearts, thereby joining his "team," or whether we want to join God's "team" by allowing Him into our hearts. And since this battle is being fought over our hearts, there is no neutral third option. We have to choose a team. So what happens when we choose?

3. The Answer

The answer to our question of why a good God would send people to Hell is remarkably simple: it's because some people choose to go there. We've already talked about how choosing to follow Jesus gives you the promise of eternal life in Heaven. And just as you can choose to follow Jesus and be granted eternal life in Heaven, you can also choose not to follow Jesus, and not to be granted eternal life in Heaven - subsequently being granted eternity in Hell instead.

Sure, no one (at least no one that I know) will legitimately say that they want to go to Hell. But the reality is that there are consequences for our choices in life, and we need to weigh those consequences before we make any choice. For example, we can choose not to go to school or not to learn a trade. The consequence would be that it will be much harder to find a good job. We can choose to eat poorly and not to exercise, but the consequence is that we'll become overweight and develop other health conditions. We can choose to enjoy a dangerous hobby like skydiving, rock climbing, or alligator wrestling, but the consequence is that we face a real risk of severe injury.

Are the risks worth it to some people? Yes - at least until they face the consequences. And I'll admit that not everyone in these examples will always face the potential ramifications, but there is a real chance that they may. However, when it comes to eternity, we're told that our eternities are *guaranteed* based on which team we choose. If we choose to follow God, we are guaranteed eternity in Heaven. If we choose not to follow God, then we have chosen to follow Satan and are guaranteed an eternity in Hell.

Let's go back to the example of the Canadian wildfires at the start of this chapter. The mandatory evacuations were broadcast everywhere, for all to see, in order to save the people from the fires. Just as the municipal authorities in Canada wanted to save people from wildfires, God wants to save us from the fires of Hell, and so He broadcasts that everywhere for all to see. John 3:16-17 says that God sent Jesus into the world to save us, not to condemn us. John 14:6 says that Jesus is the way to be saved. Romans 10:9-10 says that when we believe in our heart and confess with our mouth that Jesus is Lord, we will be saved. Isaiah chapters 52 and 53 detail the suffering that the Messiah would endure in order to save us from the penalty of our sins.

The entire Bible exists as the equivalent of an evacuation broadcast. God created Hell for Satan and the demons, and He has no desire for any of us to spend eternity there. The Bible says that God is our heavenly Father. As a father myself, I don't even want to see my daughter fall down and scrape her knee. I can't even imagine how God, a much more loving Father than I am, feels when one of his own creation chooses to leave Him for the way that leads to destruction. But, alas, the choice is ours, and as much as God warns us, He doesn't take the choice away from us. If we desire an eternity with Him, He will grant it to us, but if we desire an eternity apart from Him, He will sorrowfully grant that to us as well.

Chapter 7: If God Is Good, Why Is There So Much Suffering?

If we're honest, we all ask ourselves at times, "If God is so good, why does He allow suffering?" We've all endured some sort of pain, hardship, or adversity in our lives; some more than others. And those experiences can have a very real impact on our faith in God.

The honest truth is that everyone experiences pain and suffering, regardless of religion. Christians, Muslims, Jews, Buddhists, Atheists, and people from all other religions all know what it's like to suffer. The fact that we have pain can be a breaking point for people who are curious about any religion.

My primary goal is to give you historical, scientific, and logical evidence that prove the existence of God. The question of why suffering exists is important, but the answers to or discussion of that question don't serve as proof of the book's claim: God is real and His son died on the cross to ensure our salvation. However, it does make sense to examine, from a Christian perspective, how we can begin healing from pain with God's help.

Before we start, I'd like you to know that I believe that God has the desire and the ability to comfort us in our pain, and as I am writing this, I'm praying that He will do just that for you. The reason that I believe God wants to comfort us through our pain is because of my grandpa.

My grandpa on my mom's side of the family was a Master Sergeant in the United States Air Force. He loved his job, and was planning to serve for his entire career. However, shortly before my mom was born, his life was forever changed.

One morning, my grandpa noticed some tingling in his arms. He didn't think much of it until it continued throughout the following weeks. The tingling later appeared in his legs as well, and he began having vision issues. At this point, he knew something was wrong. He was sent to a doctor, and the doctor had a few ideas, but after several visits and many neurological tests, his primary concern was that it was Multiple Sclerosis.

Multiple Sclerosis (MS) is a disease in which the body's immune system attacks the protective lining around nerves. It can start out by causing tingling, but can eventually cause the body to deteriorate so much that the affected person may not even be able to move on their own.

This, of course, was my grandpa's greatest fear. He didn't want to leave the job that he loved because of a disease. His work was meaningful; he was proud to serve his country, and he had a family at home to take care of. But, despite his desire to continue his service, he was officially diagnosed with MS. The disease progressed quickly, and in 1976 he was medically retired.

The years that followed were some of the worst of my grandpa's life. He went from losing some functionality of his arms and legs to switching back and forth between a walker and a wheelchair. And then, only a few years after his retirement, he sat down in his wheelchair and was never able to get up on his own again.

Understandably, all of this made him extremely upset, and as the disease progressed, his anger continued to affect the family more and more, which led to him and my grandma eventually getting a divorce. It seemed for my grandpa that his suffering was going to continue to increase, until he had an encounter with the Lord.

At church one day, my grandpa decided to make Jesus his Lord and savior. And once he did, he gradually started to let go of his anger. Of course, he was still frustrated with his condition, but he allowed the Lord to change how he handled his disease. He started treating his friends and family members better. Despite the physical pain and decline of his body, my grandpa complained less and prayed more. He found an inner peace that had eluded him since his diagnosis.

Throughout the course of his life, the effects of MS would cause him to be in and out of the hospital several times. Even something as small as the common cold could land him in the hospital because of how bad his immune system was. But throughout his suffering, he continued to look to the Lord for help. And even though he was never miraculously healed from his MS, he not only lived until the age of 81, but he lived joyfully for the Lord, even leading others to God as well.

It's true that my grandpa was very familiar with suffering, but he allowed God to help him through it. And because of that, right now, he's living out the rest of eternity with his Lord, free from MS, free from pain, free from sorrow and frustration, and full of joy because of how the Lord truly saved him.

If we're going to allow God to help us through our pain like my grandpa did, we first need to have the right mindset. Many people think that God causes all of our pain, and that it's something that He does because He has a purpose that we can't see. And, while it's true that we can't always see God's purposes for us, it's wrong to think that God enjoys seeing us in pain. In fact, He's trying to rescue us from the thing that *did* cause our pain: the curse of sin.

Do you remember how we talked about Adam and Eve committing the first sin in the Garden of Eden? Well, when they did, the curse of that sin came upon the world and upon all of humanity. As a part of that curse, we are left to deal with things like natural disasters, disease, pain, sorrow, and death.

It is important to remember that suffering wasn't part of God's design. When we look back at Genesis chapters 1 and 2, we see that after each thing God created, He saw that "it was good." There was nothing wrong. It was without blemish, without defect. It was all perfect until sin entered into the picture. Sin is the broken cog in the well-oiled machine that causes issue after issue.

Picture it like this: everyone knows that Toyotas will drive forever. I've heard of Toyotas with over 500,000 miles on them, and I've personally seen some with over 300,000 that are still running. But I've also seen some die at just 150,000 miles. Why is this the case? Well, even though all Toyota owners have the instruction manuals for their vehicles in their glove boxes, not everyone takes it out. Some read it to see how they should care for their cars. They follow what is written. Others ignore it completely, saying things like, "Who needs an instruction manual for a car? I know how to drive!"

Owners who follow the maintenance instructions should have cars that run smoothly for hundreds of thousands of miles longer than average, but the owners who don't follow the instructions are taking a risk that won't pay off. (More accurately, their wallets will pay it off because they'll have to take it to the mechanic regularly or even buy another car).

In the biblical illustration, Adam and Eve had the instruction manual for life, but they didn't pay it any mind. They ignored it. They ate the forbidden fruit, invited the curse of sin into the world, and passed their proverbial broken-down Toyota down to us. And now we're left in a world that is broken down because of the curse of sin.

So where, you might ask, is God in this illustration? Well, that's the cool part. Here, God is actually the mechanic.

As I mentioned earlier in this book, my dad is a mechanic, and he can take any car and make it run again. Bad engine? No problem. He'll either fix it or find a new one and put it in. You'll never know anything was wrong with it. (I'm not exaggerating either - he's currently driving a car that had no engine at the time of the purchase.) And just like my earthly father, our Heavenly Father is a great mechanic as well. Sin broke our relationship with God, but God is offering to repair it. Sin broke the world that we live in, but our God is going to repair it back to its initial, perfect state. But why doesn't He do that right now? If God has the power to stop all of the evil and all of the pain, why doesn't He?

Ultimately, the reason is because of free will. We have the ability to choose what we want to do, and God doesn't want to take that away from us. And I'm not saying that any of us chose suffering - we sure didn't. But we can choose whether we want to follow God and allow Him to walk with us through our suffering, or if we want to wrongfully blame it on Him. Think of it this way. If your Toyota breaks down on the side of the road, you have to make a choice. Are you going to choose to try and push it to the nearest service station yourself, or are you going to choose to call roadside assistance to help you? It's up to you. And likewise, we have to make a spiritual decision. Are we going to choose to try and get through this life and all of the suffering that comes along with it on our own, or are we going to choose to call upon the name of the Lord to help us?

God wants us to call upon His name, and He wants us to love Him, but He's not going to force us to do so. Forced love isn't really love at all. So God doesn't force us, but He makes it abundantly clear that He is here, He is willing, and He is able to help us during our time on this Earth. He also says that He is offering us eternity in paradise after our time on Earth is done, and He wants as many people as possible to receive that eternity before He does away with this Earth and all of its evil.

But again, why doesn't God just end all of the evil and suffering right now? 2 Peter 3:9 says that "The Lord isn't really being slow about his promise, as some people think. No, he is being patient for your sake. He does not want anyone to be destroyed, but wants everyone to repent." Peter says that if God destroys all of the evil in this world right now, it would certainly get rid of all of the suffering that we're facing, but it also means that those who have not yet chosen to follow Jesus would be destroyed along with the evil.

God loves all people equally, so He wants as many people as possible to repent from their sins, thereby receiving His salvation, before He destroys evil. Once that happens, He *will* destroy all of the evil in the world. The book of Revelation, which is the last book in the Bible, talks extensively about how God will destroy Satan and all of the evil in this world, and about how He will destroy all suffering right along with it. The time is coming, and it's getting closer with every second. But while we're waiting for this time to come, we're still suffering. And so, we might find ourselves asking, "where is God *right now?*"

And, thank God, the Lord is near. He's not far away from you. He wants to help you through your pain. The Psalmist David wrote that "The Lord is near to the brokenhearted and saves the crushed in spirit" (Psalm 34:18 ESV), and that "Even though I walk through the valley of the shadow of death, I will fear no evil, for you are with me; your rod and your staff, they comfort me" (Psalm 23:4 ESV). Likewise, Paul wrote to the Philippians that "The Lord is near. Do not be anxious about anything, but in every situation, by prayer and petition, with thanksgiving, present your requests to God. And the peace of God, which transcends all understanding, will guard your hearts and your minds in Christ Jesus" (Philippians 4:5-7 NIV).

The truth is that God is close to us when we're suffering. God sees our pain, and He knows what it feels like as well. God had to witness the brutal death of His only Son, so He isn't a stranger to pain. But He took on that pain so that He could relate to us in our pain, and so that He could help us through it.

I'm not promising that the pain will go away the second you decide to follow God. That's not what happened for my grandpa, and I can't promise that will happen for you. But I am promising that if you follow Him, you won't have to go through your pain alone. If you're suffering, you're not alone. God has already written the story, which guarantees us that if we follow Him, the pain will indeed eventually come to an end. For me, this is one of the biggest reasons why I follow God. Whereas I used to think that He caused my pain or allowed it to happen out of ignorance or indifference, I now know that He's walking through the pain with me, and that one day, when I meet Him face to face in Heaven, He'll take it away completely and eternally.

You may not like the answer to this question, because you probably want your hardships and tribulations to go away right now. And if that's the case, welcome to the club. This is one of the main reasons why Christians always pray for Jesus to return soon - so that He'll fulfill all of the prophecies about the future, such as the one in Revelation 21 that says Jesus "...will wipe every tear from their eyes, and there will be no more death or sorrow or crying or pain. All these things are gone forever" (Revelation 21:4 NLT).

So if you're waiting for this promise, join me and all of the other Christians who are suffering in praying some of the last words of the Bible: “Amen! Come, Lord Jesus!” (Revelation 22:20b NLT).

Chapter 8: Why Do Some Christians Do Bad Things?

Some years ago, before I was a pastor, I was sharing my faith with a coworker. I was telling her about Jesus, about salvation, and about how she didn't need to try to earn her way to Heaven like she had been doing. I told her that instead, Jesus had already made a way for her.

"That all sounds great!" she said, "but I just don't think I can follow Jesus."

"Why not?" I asked. Up until this point, she had been very interested in and receptive to the message, so I thought that she might be ready to follow Jesus.

"Well, it's because I've seen way too many Christians do terrible things, and I just don't want to be associated with that crowd."

It's unfortunate, but this is a very common response people have when presented with the Gospel, and this very well may be something you're wrestling with as well. We've all heard the terrible stories about what that Catholic priest did, or who that mega-church pastor had an affair with. And it's likely that you personally know some people who call themselves Christians, although they don't act very Christ-like. All of these factors may, understandably, make you hesitant when it comes to following Jesus. I'd like to address all of these roadblocks and clarify things for you in a way that should encourage you.

To start, we'll need to remember what a "Christian" really is.

The word "Christian" literally means "little Christ." It started as a derogatory term back in the first century that was intended to offend followers of Jesus. Ironically, it ended up encouraging them, because being a "little Christ" is exactly what Christians try to do. It's kind of like if we tried making fun of a powerlifter by calling him a "giant." It would end up being a compliment because that's exactly what powerlifters are going for.

If you're trying to be a "little Christ," that means that you're following in Jesus' footsteps. You're acting the way He acted, speaking the way He spoke, and overall living the way that He lived. Now, the reality is that no one will ever be perfect at imitating Jesus, but it's all about becoming more like Him every day. So, a "Christian" is someone who has repented of their sins, asked Jesus for forgiveness, and now, does their best (with the help of the Holy Spirit) to live more like Jesus every day.

But here's the problem: *Not everyone who calls themselves a Christian really is one.* Jesus says that "Not everyone who calls out to me, 'Lord! Lord!' will enter the Kingdom of Heaven. Only those who actually do the will of my Father in heaven will enter. On judgment day many will say to me, 'Lord! Lord! We prophesied in your name and cast out demons in your name and performed many miracles in your name.' But I will reply, 'I never knew you. Get away from me, you who break God's laws'"(Matthew 7:21-23 NLT).

This means that some people will claim to be Christians their whole lives, calling Jesus their Lord, but that they never truly made Him their Lord. They just gave Him lip service. And Jesus says that this type of person won't be let into Heaven.

So the first thing that we need to realize is that the "Christians" who are doing these terrible things may not be Christians at all. They may declare that they are Christians, but Jesus certainly wouldn't agree with them. And as it's Jesus who decides ultimately who does or doesn't get to enter into Heaven, it's His opinion on the matter that's important, not ours or anyone else's.

This brings up the question: does this mean that anyone who does something bad isn't a Christian? Of course not! We're all still sinners - even when we give our lives to Jesus. But the key thing to remember is that the true Christian will repent when they do something wrong and then ask the Holy Spirit to help them refrain from it, or anything else like it, in the future. And as they grow deeper in their faith, their life will gradually begin to look more like Jesus' life. Christianity isn't about perfection, it's about moving in the right direction.

Because of this, it's also important that *we* don't try to judge whether or not someone is a true Christian. The Bible says that "people judge by outward appearance, but the LORD looks at the heart" (1 Samuel 16:7 NLT). Only God knows what's truly going on inside someone's heart, and only God can know whether someone else is truly a Christian. It is not up to us to try and make that judgement ourselves.

So, it's important to know that not everyone who calls themselves a Christian really is one. If you're choosing not to follow Jesus because of what other so-called "Christians" do, I urge you - *don't let your eternity ride on what someone else calls himself!*

However, the person who wronged you or who did something bad in general might really be a Christian. How, you may be wondering, can I ask you to follow Jesus when this other person did something so blatantly wrong? When they hurt me so much, and Jesus just forgave them?

That's a very honest and important question, and if you've been wronged or hurt by a real Christian, I want to start my answer by asking you to picture that person. Remember what they did to you. Picture their face. And now, ask yourself this question: Is this person God?

The answer is a resounding "no." I don't care who you're thinking of. Whoever it is, if there's one thing I know about them, it's that they are not God. And because they are not God, they are not perfect. They're going to do stupid stuff. They're going to hurt others. They're going to do the wrong thing. That's the reality for anyone who isn't God. I've done my own fair share of stupid stuff - I've hurt people, and I've done the wrong thing. And the reality is that you have as well. None of us are God. Only God is God, and therefore, only God is perfect. So we can't expect anyone else to be perfect, nor should they expect it of us. Not even

God expects us to be perfect. So how does God treat us as imperfect humans? He offers us grace and mercy.

It's kind of like a story my mom told me about when she was younger. When my mom was a small child, her (slightly) older cousin convinced her to ride a toy called an inchworm down a long flight of cement stairs in their grandparents' yard. She tried to, but ended up crashing down the stairs and getting a few black eyes in the process. Her cousin didn't want her to get hurt, but he did get her to do something dangerous. Should he have been punished? Or should their grandparents just immediately forgive him? Well, he actually did deserve to be punished, but instead, his grandparents showed him grace and mercy.

Mercy is when a well deserved punishment is withheld, and grace is when a blessing is given that was not earned. And, like we talked about in earlier chapters of this book, God gives us both. He shows mercy by forgiving us for our sins even though we certainly don't deserve it, and He shows grace by inviting us into Heaven when we don't deserve that either. God shows this grace to the person you're envisioning in your mind right now, and God also wants to show this grace to you, too.

Think about this: out of all the people reading this book, there's a chance that one person, when I asked them to picture someone who has done something wrong against them, thought of you. You may not remember hurting anyone, or maybe you can remember, regretfully, a handful of people you've hurt. It happens. But, you know what? God actually wants to forgive you, just as He forgave the person that *you* envisioned. But He can only forgive you if you ask Him to. *Don't let God's forgiveness of someone else prevent you from asking for His forgiveness yourself.*

To sum up the answer to the question, "Why do some Christians do bad things?" we need to remember that this world isn't perfect, and neither are the people in it. So, if you're looking to judge Christianity as a whole, it would be wrong to focus on judging the people who claim to be Christians. Even *true* Christians are not, and will never be, perfect. Jesus is the only one who is and was and ever will be perfect. Don't squander your eternity by focusing on the sins of others and refusing to ask for your own forgiveness. Remember, "[God] will judge everyone according to what they have done. He will give eternal life to those who keep on doing good, seeking after the glory and honor and immortality that God offers. But he will pour out his anger and wrath on those who live for themselves, who refuse to obey the truth and instead live lives of wickedness" (Romans 2:6-8 NLT).

God wants our focus to be on Jesus. So instead, look at the life, words, and teachings of Jesus, and let that be the only determining factor for whether or not you want to follow Him.

Section 4: The Preview

You've seen a lot of evidence for Christianity, you know what it's all about, and you've gotten over some hangups, but will anything change when you become a Christian? In this final section, we'll take a look at what it looks like to follow Jesus.

Could It Be True?

Chapter 9: Count the Cost

At this point, we've talked about the proof that God exists, proved that the Bible is a historically accurate document, and proved that Jesus rose from the dead. You know why Christianity is important, and you know why it is the one true religion. And finally, we've cleared up some of the most common objections to Christianity. You may be ready to give your life to Jesus, and that's amazing! But, before you do, we have one final point. Aside from knowing that Jesus is the only way to receive forgiveness for our sins, it is the most important point yet: counting the cost of Christianity.

While it's true that salvation is a free gift from God and that we don't need to pay for it or earn it in any way, there is a cost to Christianity. And this cost comes from the world. You see, when you give your life to Jesus, you're giving up your old way of life and becoming a different person. As much as God loves that, the world hates it. Satan hates it. And Satan will do whatever he can to get you to fall away from Christ and to start following the ways of the world again.

Jesus speaks about this reality in what is known as "The Parable of the Sower". Take a look at what He says:

> A sower went out to sow. And as he sowed, some seeds fell along the path, and the birds came and devoured them. Other seeds fell on rocky ground, where they did not have much soil, and immediately they sprang up, since they had no depth of soil, but when the sun rose they were scorched. And since they had no root, they withered away. Other seeds fell among thorns, and the thorns grew up and choked them. Other seeds fell on good soil and produced grain, some a hundredfold, some sixty, some thirty. He who has ears, let him hear (Matthew 13:3b-9 ESV).

In this parable, Jesus talks about four different types of people, each represented by seeds. First, He mentions that some seeds fall along the path, and are devoured by birds. This represents people who hear the message of Christ, but just as the seeds never sprout, their faith never sprouts, and they never make Jesus their Lord and Savior.

Second, Jesus talks about the seed that falls on the rocky ground. These seeds spring up, representing some people who choose to follow Christ. But the seeds wither away quickly, representing how some people fall away from Christianity just as quickly as they embrace it.

Third, Jesus talks about the seeds that fall among the thorns. This represents people who embrace Christ as Lord and Savior, but when they are persecuted, their faith dies, just as a sprout dies when surrounded by thorns.

Finally, Jesus talks about the seeds that fall in the good soil. These represent the people who make Jesus their Lord and Savior and who stay strong in their faith throughout their entire life.

Jesus wants us all to be the seed that falls in the good soil. He wants us to have faith that endures, despite any persecution that may come our way. And in order to have that kind of faith, you'll need to know what's coming your way, and you'll need to know how Jesus is stronger than all of it.

There are three challenges that we'll face when we become Christians. We'll face loss - we need to leave certain things behind when we choose to follow Jesus.

We'll face persecution for following Jesus, and we'll face opposition from Satan when we choose to follow Jesus. We will dissect all three of these things for two reasons: First, I want to let you know about what's in store for those who accept Christ, and second, because I also want to give you reassurance and hope. Each of these challenges is temporary, and the reward we will receive for facing them is eternal. Let's dive in.

We will face loss.

In the book of 1 John, we're told that we'll eventually lose everything in our lives that is "worldly." The apostle John writes:

> Do not love this world nor the things it offers you, for when you love the world, you do not have the love of the Father in you. For the world offers only a craving for physical pleasure, a craving for everything we see, and pride in our achievements and possessions. These are not from the Father, but are from this world. And this world is fading away, along with everything that people crave. But anyone who does what pleases God will live forever (1 John 2:15-17 NLT).

Here, we're clearly told not to focus on worldly things, which are defined as things that satisfy our "craving for pleasure," our "craving for everything we see," and "pride in our achievements and possessions." In this world, we're often taught that our success and happiness both come from physical possessions, titles, accumulation of wealth, and academic and professional performance. And while we may enjoy these things, to focus on them entirely is a mistake, because, as we read in 1 John, we'll lose all of them when we enter into Heaven. Not only will they become unimportant, they'll also be non-existent.

Instead, we're told as followers of Jesus to do what pleases God so that instead of accumulating worldly prizes that we will eventually lose, we can store up eternal rewards that will never fade away. When speaking on eternal rewards, Jesus tells us, "Don't store up treasures here on earth, where moths eat them and rust destroys them, and where thieves break in and steal. Store your treasures in heaven, where moths and rust cannot destroy, and thieves do not break in and steal" (Matthew 6:19-20 NLT).

Contrary to the loss we'll face as Christians, the prospect of receiving eternal rewards is very encouraging! So how do we focus on earning these eternal rewards?

We do this through what the Bible calls "Losing our life."

In the book of Matthew, Jesus says, "Whoever finds his life will lose it, and whoever loses his life for my sake will find it" (Matthew 10:39 ESV). What is Jesus saying here?

Jesus isn't saying that we need to lose our life in a literal sense. Rather, He's saying that we need to live a life of obedience and surrender to God, and we need to commit to turning from our sins, or losing them, whatever those sins may be. In 1 Thessalonians, the apostle Paul clarifies Jesus' teaching by saying that "God has called us to live holy lives, not impure lives. Therefore, anyone who refuses to live by these rules is not disobeying human teaching but is rejecting God, who gives his Holy Spirit to you" (1 Thessalonians 4:7-8 NLT). Here, Paul implies that there will be things that the world says are perfectly fine, but that God says are sins. Perhaps the most common examples of these things today are things like swearing, coarse jokes, gossip, slander (speaking negatively about someone behind their back in a way that hurts their reputation), lying, and sexual sin (which is defined repeatedly in the Bible as any sexual activity outside of a marriage between a man and a woman). Many of these things are acceptable in the eyes of the world, but for those who follow Jesus, we're called to leave these things behind.

And as hard as it may be to leave our sins behind, we will receive abundant rewards in Heaven when we choose to lose them!

Ultimately, we are called to focus on things that are eternal, rather than on things that are of this Earth. Remember, God's main focus isn't on our earthly lives, it's on our eternal lives. Because of this, we know that God has so much more in store for us in Heaven than we could even imagine here. So, as Christians, let's leave our sins behind and live holy lives. And let's take heart in the promise that any sin, possession, title, or otherwise that we leave behind will be left in favor of eternal rewards that are far greater than anything we could ever lose.

We will face persecution.

The second thing we'll face as followers of Jesus is persecution. We're told this in several verses throughout the Bible, such as in Paul's letter to Timothy, where he says, "Yes, and everyone who wants to live a godly life in Christ Jesus will suffer persecution" (2 Timothy 3:12 NLT).

Persecution can come in many forms. If you're in the United States like me, you'll likely only ever face verbal persecution. This is when people criticize you, gossip about you, or slander you for being a Christian.

You will likely lose friendships because of your decision to follow Jesus, because it means that your mindset will transform to become more like Jesus', whereas you used to follow the world. I've been through this personally, because once I gave my life to Jesus, I no longer agreed with the lifestyle one of my friends was living. Even though I didn't criticize her for living this lifestyle (knowing that she wasn't a Christian herself), she knew that I didn't support it and so she didn't want to associate with me any longer. But thankfully, persecution like this has been the only persecution I've faced.

In many parts of the world, Christians are physically persecuted. Becoming a Christian may ostracize you from your family. In some places it could lead you to be beaten, imprisoned, or even killed. All of Jesus' apostles were physically persecuted for their faith, and many of them were killed because of it. And unfortunately, the persecution hasn't lightened up in the past 2000 years. There are several countries in the world where Christianity is illegal, and each year, thousands of people are killed specifically because they are Christians.[19]

---

[19] APPG for International Freedom of Religion or Belief, How Many Christians Are Killed Each Year Because of Their Faith?, accessed April 12, 2025, https://appgfreedomofreligionorbelief.org/how-many-christians-are-killed-each-year-because-of-their-faith/

Jesus spoke a great deal about persecution during His ministry, which makes sense, because He was persecuted Himself, to the point that He was killed for claiming to be the Messiah (even though it was true). But when we see what Jesus said about persecution, He actually spoke about it in a very encouraging way. Let's take a look at a few things Jesus said on this topic:

I. Jesus says that when we're persecuted, it's not because we're doing something wrong - it's because of Him: "If the world hates you, remember that it hated me first. The world would love you as one of its own if you belonged to it, but you are no longer part of the world. I chose you to come out of the world, so it hates you. Do you remember what I told you? 'A slave is not greater than the master.' Since they persecuted me, naturally they will persecute you. And if they had listened to me, they would listen to you. They will do all this to you because of me, for they have rejected the one who sent me" (John 15:18-21 NLT).

II. Jesus says that persecution should be expected, but it is rewarded: "And all nations will hate you because you are my followers. But everyone who endures to the end will be saved" (Matthew 10:22 NLT). Likewise, in Matthew 5:11-12 (NLT), He says, "God blesses you when people mock you and persecute you and lie about you and say all sorts of evil things against you because you are my followers. Be happy about it! Be very glad! For a great reward awaits you in heaven. And remember, the ancient prophets were persecuted in the same way."

III. Through Paul, He encourages us, teaching us that nothing can separate us from His love:

Can anything ever separate us from Christ's love? Does it mean he no longer loves us if we have trouble or calamity, or are persecuted, or hungry, or destitute, or in danger, or threatened with death? (As the Scriptures say, "For your sake we are killed every day; we are being slaughtered like sheep.") No, despite all these things, overwhelming victory is ours through Christ, who loved us. And I am convinced that nothing can ever separate us from God's love. Neither death nor life, neither

> angels nor demons, neither our fears for today nor our worries about tomorrow—not even the powers of hell can separate us from God's love. No power in the sky above or in the earth below—indeed, nothing in all creation will ever be able to separate us from the love of God that is revealed in Christ Jesus our Lord (Romans 8:35-39 NLT).

While we're counting the cost of Christianity, we need to know that persecution should be expected. But we also need to know that, if we stand strong in our faith through persecution, having eternity in Heaven with Jesus will make any persecution we face worth it.

We will face opposition from Satan.

When we give our lives to Jesus, it's a major victory for Heaven, but it's a major defeat for Satan. Satan wants nothing more than to keep us from a relationship with Jesus. So, even if we do give our lives to Jesus despite the pressure Satan puts on us, Satan will simply focus on "breaking us up" with Jesus instead.

Satan has several tactics to do this. He even tried to employ some of them on Jesus! In Matthew 4:1-4, we see Satan try to tempt Jesus into sin by getting Him to focus on worldly things. Jesus was fasting, and Satan tried to convince Jesus to use His power as the Son of God to turn some rocks into bread. Jesus was physically able to do this, but as the purpose of fasting is to help you connect with God and hunger for Him spiritually, He knew that Satan was trying to shift Jesus' focus from God to food.

Next, Satan tried to tempt Jesus into sin by misquoting scripture in verses 5-7. He tells Jesus that the scriptures say that God would send His angels to protect Jesus so He would never be hurt. Then, he told Jesus to prove the scriptures by jumping off the highest point of the Temple. While the scriptures do say that God would send His angels to protect Jesus, Jesus knew that this was not the context in which the scriptures were written.

Finally, Satan tries to tempt Jesus into worshiping him by offering Jesus power. Satan said that he would give Jesus all of the kingdoms of the world if only He would bow down to worship him. Again, Jesus resisted.

These are merely a few of the tactics Satan used on Jesus in an attempt to lead Him away from God, and he will try everything he can to lead us away from God as well. Maybe he'll have someone misquote scripture to you in a way that makes you question your faith.

Maybe he tells you that you're not worth God's love. Maybe he sends people to persecute you. Maybe he tries to lure you away with physical possessions or money or influence or power. Maybe he tries something completely different.

What's key is to be ready for Satan to try to get you back to his side. If he tried to tear the Son of God Himself away from God, then he'll definitely try to tear us away from Him. And when he does try, what do we do? We call upon God's Truth, just like Jesus did. In Ephesians 6:11-18, Paul teaches us how to call upon God's Truth when Satan attacks:

> Put on all of God's armor so that you will be able to stand firm against all strategies of the devil. For we are not fighting against flesh-and-blood enemies, but against evil rulers and authorities of the unseen world, against mighty powers in this dark world, and against evil spirits in the heavenly places. Therefore, put on every piece of God's armor so you will be able to resist the enemy in the time of evil. Then after the battle you will still be standing firm. Stand your ground, putting on the belt of truth and the body armor of God's righteousness. For shoes, put on the peace that comes from the Good News so that you will be fully prepared. In addition to all

> of these, hold up the shield of faith to stop the fiery arrows of the devil. Put on salvation as your helmet, and take the sword of the Spirit, which is the word of God. Pray in the Spirit at all times and on every occasion. Stay alert and be persistent in your prayers for all believers everywhere. (Ephesians 6:11-18 NLT).

Churches around the world have dissected this passage and have provided sermon series that span months around what it looks like to "put on the armor of God" because of how rich and practical this text is. But, for our purposes, let's just get a general overview of what it looks like to put on the armor of God.

First, we need to recognize our enemy. Paul says that we aren't fighting against flesh and blood, meaning that it's not a fight against a human. Our fight is against Satan. One of Satan's greatest tricks is to trick people into thinking he doesn't exist. Only through recognizing the fact that Satan is our true enemy can we resist him.

Next, we're told to put on the whole armor of God. This isn't physical armor, Paul is using armor as a metaphor as he teaches us how we should arm ourselves spiritually, just as soldiers arm themselves physically. Let's look at each piece of "armor" and its significance:

The belt of truth: We need to remember the truth that Jesus is the Son of God and has given us salvation as a free gift. This is the truth that we're fighting for, and just as your armor will fall apart without a belt, so our spiritual defense will fall apart if we forget this truth.

The body armor of God's righteousness: Like body armor protects us physically, God's righteousness protects us spiritually. We've received the very righteousness of God when we made Jesus our Lord and Savior, so God doesn't see us as dirty sinners anymore. Instead, He sees us as His redeemed children. When Satan attacks us with shame and guilt and doubt, it's the body armor of God's righteousness that will protect us.

The shoes of the peace that comes from the Good News: Just as shoes provide comfort when walking long distances, we can have comfort and peace during the fight against Satan because we remember the Good News that we've been forgiven and redeemed through Christ.

The shield of faith: One of Satan's tactics is to get us to doubt Jesus. But faith is stronger than doubt, so by holding up the shield of faith, we can be protected against this attack.

The helmet of salvation: A helmet guards your brain, so when we put on the helmet of salvation, we're allowing the assurance of our salvation to guard our mind against fear, doubt, and discouragement.

The sword of the Spirit: The sword of the Spirit is the Word of God. This is how we attack. Each time Jesus was tempted by Satan in Matthew 4, He attacked Satan right back by quoting scripture. Likewise, when we memorize scripture as Jesus did, we're training to be able to not only protect ourselves from Satan's attacks, but also to call upon the Lord, who is much stronger than Satan, in our own temptation.

To end this passage of scripture, Paul tells us to "Stay alert." Just as a watchman stays alert for an enemy attack, we need to stay alert for a spiritual attack. When we're always expecting spiritual opposition, we're always ready to fend it off. So, like Paul, I encourage you to put on the whole armor of God and to stay alert!

Admittedly, the cost of following Jesus is very high. But, I hope you now know that the reward far exceeds the cost. We may need to give up the world in order to follow Jesus, but in return, we're receiving eternal life and rewards. We may be persecuted for our faith, but the persecution will only be temporary, and our life in Heaven with Jesus will be eternal. And we will face spiritual opposition, but Jesus helps us to protect ourselves with the armor of God and with the assurance of our salvation.

Chapter 10: The Invitation

We've taken quite the journey together throughout the pages of this book. We've seen lots of evidence that points to a God that loves us so much that He gave His only Son up for us, saving us from the penalty of our sins. But simply being able to prove God's existence and explain salvation isn't the main point of Christianity. We need to take action on what we now know. And so, there's one final question that I have for you, and I hope you'll answer it honestly: At this point in your life, what's stopping you from following Jesus?

Maybe you still have some questions about Christianity that you would like to be answered. If so, join the club! There are still many questions that I don't have answers to, as well. But I know enough about God that I was willing to put my faith in Him - even without having all of the answers. I encourage you to take that step of faith, just like I did, and make Jesus your Lord and Savior.

If you have read this book and are now ready to put your faith in Jesus, I'm so excited for you! I can't promise that everything will be made easier when you put your faith in Jesus - in fact, Jesus Himself says that we'll still have struggles on this side of eternity, even if we follow Him. I do know, however, that when you put your faith in Jesus, your eternity will change! Since you are ready to accept Jesus into your heart, let me answer one final question about Christianity that is likely still burning in your mind:

What Is Heaven Like?

The apostle John was given a vision of Heaven, which he described in the last book of the Bible, Revelation. Here's what he wrote:

> I heard a loud shout from the throne, saying, "Look, God's home is now among his people! He will live with them, and they will be his people. God himself will be with them. He will wipe every tear from their eyes, and there will be no more death or sorrow or crying or pain. All these

> things are gone forever." And the one sitting on the throne said, "Look, I am making everything new!" And then he said to me, "Write this down, for what I tell you is trustworthy and true." And he also said, "It is finished! I am the Alpha and the Omega—the Beginning and the End. To all who are thirsty I will give freely from the springs of the water of life. All who are victorious will inherit all these blessings, and I will be their God, and they will be my children" (Revelation 21:3-7 NLT).

Imagine an eternity with no suffering. No pain. No tears. A perfect paradise, created for us by God, our Father, who loves us so much that He gave up everything so that we might get to spend eternity with Him. This, my friends, is Heaven. I'm so glad that I'm going to get to experience this, and I'm so glad that God has given you the opportunity to experience it, too.

If your mind is made up, and if you'd like to ask Jesus to be your Lord and your Savior, all you need to do is ask Him to be. Just pray to God, giving Him your heart. The words you pray don't matter; it's not the prayer that saves you. It's your heart that matters. So, just express your heart to God. If you've never prayed before, feel free to pray something like this in your own words:

Heavenly Father,
Thank you for revealing yourself to me, and for showing me the truth that even though I'm a sinner, you love me so much that you gave up your Son so that I could be forgiven. I ask for your forgiveness, and I thank you that even though there's nothing I could ever do to deserve it, it makes you happier than anything to forgive me anyway. I now believe that Jesus is the Son of God, and so, with joy filling my heart, I accept His sacrifice as payment for my sins. Thank you for saving me and for giving me the promise of eternal life in Heaven. Please help me to learn about you, serve you, and honor you throughout the rest of my life. I pray in Jesus' name,
Amen.

Congratulations on joining God's family and entering into His Kingdom!

- Jack

What's Next?

To take the next step in your faith journey, visit
www.methuselahco.com

Acknowledgements

This book wouldn't exist without the people God has placed in my life. My dad has been a steady example of love and sacrifice for as long as I can remember - from working extra hours when I was little so my mom could stay home with me, to showing up time and time again to help with whatever I need, and it's an honor to dedicate this book to him. My wife, Lizzy, has been a constant source of encouragement, faithfully taking care of Emilie while I spent long hours writing. I'm also grateful to my mom, as well as Andrew and Nick, who spent lots of time and energy to help sharpen this book, to Jake, for creating an amazing cover design, to Robby, whose encouragement meant more than he knows, and to Mike, whose investment in teaching me how to study the Bible has had a lasting impact on both me and this work. And above all, I'm thankful for Jesus, whose grace made this possible and who allows me to play even a small part in His Kingdom.

Bibliography

Chapter 1:

1. American Museum of Natural History. "Georges Lemaître: Father of the Big Bang." *American Museum of Natural History*. Accessed April 12, 2025. https://www.amnh.org/learn-teach/curriculum-collections/cosmic-horizons-book/georges-lemaitre-big-bang.
2. Answers in Genesis. "Does the Big Bang Fit with the Bible?" Last modified February 29, 2012. Accessed April 12, 2025. https://answersingenesis.org/big-bang/.
3. Rhodes, Ron. *The Big Book of Bible Answers: A Guide to Understanding the Most Challenging Questions.* Eugene, OR: Harvest House Publishers, 2013.
4. MacArthur, John. "ChristoCreation: Christ as Creation's Eternal Word, Light of Man, and Source of Technological Wisdom." *The Master's University News*. Accessed August 30, 2025. https://www.masters.edu/master_tmu_news/john-macarthur-christocreation-theotech-2021.
5. NASA Goddard Space Flight Center. 2020. "What Makes a Planet Habitable?" NASA

Science Exploration and Climate Change. Accessed April 13, 2025. https://seec.gsfc.nasa.gov/what_makes_a_planet_habitable.html.

6. Lunar and Planetary Institute. *Habitability Reference Table.* Houston, TX: Lunar and Planetary Institute. Accessed April 12, 2025. https://www.lpi.usra.edu/education/explore/our_place/hab_ref_table.pdf.
7. NASA. "Life in the Universe: What Are the Odds?" Accessed April 12, 2025. https://science.nasa.gov/universe/exoplanets/life-in-the-universe-what-are-the-odds/.
8. Hoyle, Fred. *The Intelligent Universe.* London: Michael Joseph, 1983.
9. Wallace, J. Warner. *God's Crime Scene: A Cold-Case Detective Examines the Evidence for a Divinely Created Universe.* Colorado Springs: David C. Cook, 2015.
10. United States Holocaust Memorial Museum. *Dietrich Bonhoeffer.* Holocaust Encyclopedia. Accessed August 30, 2025. https://encyclopedia.ushmm.org/content/en/article/dietrich-bonhoeffer.
11. Heschel, Abraham Joshua. Quoted in *Jewish Virtual Library.* "Quotations on the Holocaust." Accessed August 30, 2025.

https://www.jewishvirtuallibrary.org/quotations-on-the-holocaust.

12. Gandhi, Mahatma. *Letter to Adolf Hitler.* July 23, 1939. In *Selected Letters of Mahatma Gandhi.* Accessed August 30, 2025. https://www.mkgandhi.org/letters/hitler_ltr1.php .

Chapter 2

1. Stoner, Peter W. *Science Speaks.* Chicago: Moody Press, 1963.
2. Albright, William F. *The Archaeology of Palestine.* Harmondsworth, Middlesex: Penguin Books, 1960.
3. Grant, Michael. *Jesus: An Historian's Review of the Gospels.* New York: Macmillan, 1977.
4. Ramsay, Sir William Mitchell. *St. Paul the Traveller and the Roman Citizen.* London: Hodder and Stoughton, 1904. Accessed via Christian Classics Ethereal Library. https://www.ccel.org/ccel/ramsay/paul_roman/paul_roman.iv.html.

Chapter 3

1. Josephus, Flavius. *Antiquities of the Jews*. Translated by William Whiston. Peabody, MA: Hendrickson Publishers, 1987.
2. Josephus, Flavius. *Antiquities of the Jews*. Translated by William Whiston. Peabody, MA: Hendrickson Publishers, 1987.
3. Pliny the Younger. *The Letters of the Younger Pliny*. Translated by Betty Radice. London: Penguin Books, 1969.
4. Lewis, C.S. *Mere Christianity*. New York: HarperOne, 2001.
5. Habermas, Gary R., and Michael R. Licona. *The Case for the Resurrection of Jesus*. Grand Rapids, MI: Kregel Publications, 2004.
6. Edwards, William D., Wesley J. Gabel, and Floyd E. Hosmer. "On the Physical Death of Jesus Christ." *Journal of the American Medical Association* 255, no. 11 (1986): 1455–63. https://lehighvalleychurch.com/wp-content/uploads/2020/04/Medical-Account-of-the-Crucifixion-.pdf.

Chapter 5

1. Grudem, Wayne. *Systematic Theology: An Introduction to Biblical Doctrine.* Grand Rapids, MI: Zondervan, 1994.
2. Fishbane, Michael. *Judaism: Revelation and Traditions.* San Francisco: Harper & Row, 1987.
3. The Jewish Publication Society. *Tanakh: The Holy Scriptures.* Philadelphia: JPS, 1985.
4. Rahman, Fazlur. *Major Themes of the Qur'an.* 2nd ed. Chicago: University of Chicago Press, 2009.
5. The Qur'an. Translated by M.A.S. Abdel Haleem. Oxford: Oxford University Press, 2005.
6. Keown, Damien. *Buddhism: A Very Short Introduction.* Oxford: Oxford University Press, 1996.
7. *The Dhammapada.* Translated by Eknath Easwaran. Tomales, CA: Nilgiri Press, 2007.
8. Flood, Gavin. *The Bhagavad Gita: A New Translation.* New York: W. W. Norton & Company, 2012.
9. Embree, Ainslie T. *The Hindu Tradition: Readings in Oriental Thought.* New York: Random House, 1972.
10. Radhakrishnan, Sarvepalli. *The Hindu View of Life.* Oxford University Press, 1990.

11. Harvey, Peter. *An Introduction to Buddhism: Teachings, History and Practices.* 2nd ed. Cambridge: Cambridge University Press, 2013.
12. Eck, Diana L. *Darsan: Seeing the Divine Image in India.* 3rd ed. New York: Columbia University Press, 1998.
13. Zaehner, R. C. *Hinduism.* Oxford: Oxford University Press, 1962.

Chapter 9:

1. APPG for International Freedom of Religion or Belief. *How Many Christians Are Killed Each Year Because of Their Faith?* Accessed April 12, 2025. https://appgfreedomofreligionorbelief.org/how-many-christians-are-killed-each-year-because-of-their-faith/.

About the Author

Jack Duga serves as a pastor at New Day Church in Enfield, Connecticut, where he is especially passionate about engaging with the difficult questions surrounding God, faith, and doubt. He believes honest questions deserve honest answers, and that clarity matters when belief feels uncertain. Jack lives in Connecticut with his wife, Lizzy, and their daughter.

www.ingramcontent.com/pod-product-compliance
Lightning Source LLC
LaVergne TN
LVHW090516110826
845146LV00003B/881
* 9 7 9 8 9 9 5 2 5 8 5 1 3 *